Making Patterns *from* Finished Clothes

Written and illustrated by

RUSTY BENSUSSEN

Sterling Publishing Co., Inc.   New York

ACKNOWLEDGMENTS

No book happens by itself and no author can claim to have written that book without the aid of many people. I tender appreciation and gratitude to Ed Bensussen, my husband, my mentor and my patron; Gayle Carrol and Wendy Walls, my two wonderful daughters; Michelle Verlander, Caryl Weldon and Floss Tanzer, friends, teachers and critics; Lou Doyle, my first editor; and Claire Shaeffer, author, who gave freely of her professional expertise.

Library of Congress Cataloging in Publication Data

Bensussen, Rusty.
  Making patterns from finished clothes.

  Includes index.
  1. Dressmaking—Pattern design.   I. Title.
TT520.B48   1985   646.4'072   84-26763
ISBN 0-8069-5704-2
ISBN 0-8069-7978-X (pbk.)

Published by Sterling Publishing Company, Inc.
387 Park Avenue South, New York, N.Y. 10016
© 1985 by Estelle Bensussen
Distributed in Canada by Sterling Publishing
% Canadian Manda Group, P.O. Box 920, Station U
Toronto, Ontario, Canada M8Z 5P9
Distributed in Great Britain and Europe by Cassell PLC
Villiers House, 41/47 Strand, London WC2N 5JE, England
Distributed in Australia by Capricorn Link Ltd.
P.O. Box 665, Lane Cove, NSW 2066
Manufactured in the United States of America

CONTENTS

Preface   5

Organizing   7

Equipment • Filing Patterns • Pattern Notebook

Fashions, Fabrics & Figure Types   9

Silhouettes, Line & Space • Color • Fabrics • Figure Types

DRAFTING PATTERNS   23
Clothes with Capped Sleeves   25

Choosing a Garment • Survey • Back • Coding the Patterns • Front •
Inseam Pockets • Using Your Pattern Creatively • Kimono Sleeve •
At-Home Robe • More Ideas • Nightgown • Pull-on Pants

Clothes with Set-in Sleeves   45

Choosing a Garment • Survey • Back • Sleeve • Coding the Patterns •
Using Your Pattern Creatively • Windbreaker • Pullover Jacket •
Unlined Coat • Reversible Coat • Long or Short Dresses • Direct-Cut
Method and Additional Thoughts

Skirts   63

Survey • Step 1—Back • Step 2—Front • Wrap Skirts • A-Line Skirts •
Dirndl Skirts • Tulip Skirts • Gored Skirts • Pleats • Godets • Alterations • Using Your Pattern Creatively

Pants   103

Choosing a Garment • Survey • Front: Knits • Back: Knits • Patch Pockets • Woven Pants • Survey • Front • Back • Using Your Pattern Creatively • Trousers • Cropped Pants • Wrap Pants • Palazzo Pants • Drawstrings • Sweat Pants • Athletic Shorts • Short Shorts • Jamaicas • Bermudas • Culottes

The Ultimate Pattern   143

Dresses • Tent Dress • Shirtwaist Dress • Jumpsuit • Jumpsuit: Knit Fabrics • Jumpsuit with Center-Front Seam • Jumpsuit with Waistline Seam • Jumpsuit: Woven Fabric • Bib Overalls

Index   157

PREFACE

We all have clothes in our wardrobes that are such a joy to wear that we wish we had them in twenty different fabrics and in every color of the rainbow. But when this garment (dress or skirt, shorts or pants) is no longer available in the local stores, and there does not seem to be a commercial pattern that comes close to the original style, what can you do? The answer is simple: Cut your own pattern directly from the existing garment and you will soon be enjoying that fashion in *your* choice of colors and fabrics.

There is no mystery to cutting patterns from finished clothes or in using a skirt or pants or another garment as a pattern. With these easy-to-follow instructions, you will be able to duplicate almost anything in your wardrobe without taking myriad measurements. Nor will you have to take apart a garment that you are still wearing. You will be led through a step-by-step learning experience as you would in a classroom. But with this book you can travel at your own pace, review at your convenience and take as much or as little time for each project as you desire—with your personal tutor always at hand.

This is not a basic sewing book. It contains no instructions on taking up a hem or threading a sewing machine. Instead, this book gives you the basic know-how to draft an assortment of patterns from garments in your closet, your neighbor's wardrobe, your imagination or anywhere you might find a design that pleases you. For the individual with basic sewing skills who cannot get beyond a commercial pattern to create her or his own designs and ideas—this is a perfect system.

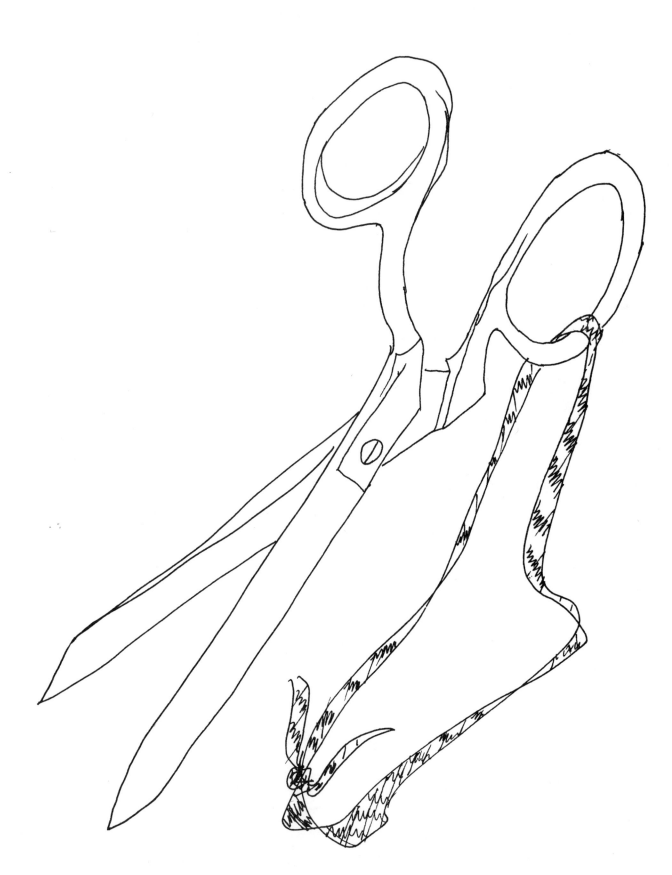

ORGANIZING

Equipment

The nicest thing about making your own patterns is that there is no need to purchase additional equipment. In the past, my new projects needed many additional items that I might or might not ever use again after I had completed the project.

Pattern drafting has renewed my faith in do-it-yourself! The required equipment is what you'll find among your sewing supplies. This is all you need:

Roll of newsprint *or*
Roll of brown wrapping paper *or* tissue paper *or*
Yesterday's newspaper (optional) *or*
Nonwoven bonded textiles (explained below, optional)
Yardstick
Tape measure
2 soft-tipped or ball-point pens of different colors
Transparent tape
Pins
Scissors or shears

If you prefer, use one of the pattern-drafting substitutes, such as Do-Sew (made by Stretch & Sew), Stacy's Tracer (made by Stacy Fabrics), Pattern Tracing Cloth (made by Staple Sewing Aids Corp.) or Pellon nonwoven bonded textiles, instead of the paper, to make your patterns. These nonwoven textiles make the patterns far more permanent. They won't tear easily and any wrinkles are easily smoothed with a warm iron.

Filing Patterns

Long ago I learned that filing pattern pieces on the cutting board or sewing table assured my not finding them again when I later wanted to use the patterns. After much stewing over lost pattern sections, I bought a letter-sized, four-drawer, filing cabinet of pasteboard. Several packages of 8- by 10-inch (20.3- by 25.4-cm) manila envelopes completed my purchase, and I began organizing the sewing room.

These purchases really didn't make too much of a "neatnik" of me. But I no longer have to conduct scavenger hunts to find pattern instruction sheets or devise maps for getting around in my sewing room. Every pattern now has its own home: an envelope where I have drawn a quick sketch of the garment on the front, noted the date, my size and weight, type of garment and yardage requirements for the original creation. On the back, I write details of any revisions. The pattern pieces, folded together, are in the envelope that fits neatly into the file drawer. These originals can easily be interspersed with commercial patterns.

File dividers will help you locate your stored patterns in the cabinet. The envelopes can either be coded by numbers or divided into style groups. The method obviously will be your personal choice, but first, consider dividing your patterns by *style*. It's much easier to find a pants pattern, for instance, among a group of pants patterns than to look through an entire file drawer because you can't remember the pattern number.

Since most of the patterns I purchased are of the "designer" variety, the envelopes are about the same size as those in my file. They are interspersed with my own patterns, and are equally visible.

Non-designer patterns are usually distributed in smaller envelopes. Removing the patterns from these little envelopes is easy, but replacing them without tearing the pattern and envelope becomes a monumental task. My solution to this problem: cut around the outside edges of these small envelopes and rubber-cement or tape the front and back to either side of the larger envelopes (fig. 1). It makes the replacement of all the pattern pieces so much easier. Now, I automatically put away a pattern immediately after use. I'm no longer short one sleeve pattern or missing an instruction sheet when reusing commercial patterns. I preserve the entire original envelope and its contents.

fig. 1

Smaller envelopes can be used, but they do create one minor problem—you must make additional folds in your pattern pieces. When using envelopes smaller than those I suggested above, iron each pattern piece before you use it, if the creases don't shake out when the pattern is removed from the envelope. A crease left in a pattern piece is like a fold made to reduce the size of that piece. The finished garment can't fit properly if the pattern is too small.

Pattern Notebook

Creating a pattern notebook is a very wise move: 1) it stores a wealth of elusive information at your fingertips; 2) it is a valuable aid when shopping in your favorite fabric store; 3) it becomes a handy index to your pattern file.

Buy a small loose-leaf notebook that fits into your purse. Devote a separate page (or more, if needed) to each pattern that you have drafted. Copy the sketch that you made for the pattern envelope, note

the date, your measurements and/or your dress size, just as you wrote it on your pattern. Indicate the type of fabric (knitted or woven), yardage (amount of fabric needed) and list all notions (zipper, buttons, hem binding, etc.). Glue or tape swatches of the fabric to the same page. Detail all revisions, if any, of the original pattern and attach additional swatches of fabric from any new versions you may have made (fig. 2).

Your pattern notebook will not only serve as an index to the pattern file, but also as a guide and convenience when shopping for fabrics and notions. You will easily coordinate textures and colors without the burden of carrying finished garments to the fabric store. Your new notebook will also remind you to buy important notions for the style you are working on. Since your notions list will now be with you when you leave home, all purchases can be made at the same time.

Over the years, many brilliant designs, noted on the insides of matchbook covers, were lost. Now, my little pattern book is a permanent place to note ideas and sketches for future pattern revisions and new designs. Yours can serve you as well and be a real asset.

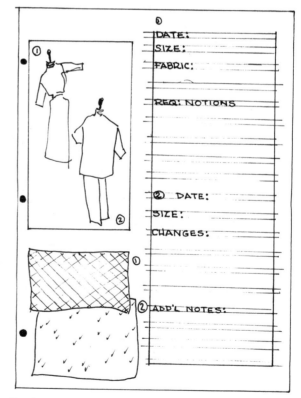

fig. 2

FASHIONS, FABRICS & FIGURE TYPES

There really are no hard and fast rules governing the choice of fabric. Colors and textures are purely personal choices. Fibres used in unique ways are almost impossible to identify. There was once a time when fabrics were considered seasonal: cotton was a summer fabric; velvet was worn only in winter; etc. In today's fashion scene, fabric spans all seasons and multiple occasions. Personal taste becomes the latest word in fashion. New methods now used for weaving and knitting fabrics and the blending of yarns have made seasonal classification a thing of the past. A blend of three or more traditionally "summer" fibres, such as linen, cotton and rayon, could produce a fabric suitable for a New England winter. On the other hand, I have chosen some wools (traditionally "winter" fabrics) that are like gossamer. Clothes from these wonderful wools have kept me cool through the heat of summer.

Long ago, I had a sweeping, gored skirt of Harris tweed liberally sprinkled with rhinestones. I loved it because it was a total contradiction—the combination shocked some of my less imaginative acquaintances. But it made me happy when I wore it; it was my personal choice. I also enjoyed a pantsuit of grey, black and metallic silver plaid that I wore primarily on the golf course. The fabric could have been at home in the theatre or the opera, but the style was pure sportswear—again, my personal choice. You don't have to conform to "the uniform of the day." Have faith in your choice and enjoy it.

Proportion, which we will discuss in depth later in this chapter, will dictate your final fabric and pattern choices, but don't be talked out of a fabric or design because your friend doesn't think *she* can wear it. The choices you make are for *you*—your personal expression, your personal look.

You must be very honest with yourself when you sew. If you buy the wrong dress you can return it for cash or credit and purchase another style. If you sew the wrong dress, you have lost the fabric, the time and the money. You can avoid pitfalls by knowing yourself—your taste and figure type.

Silhouettes, Line & Space

We should have a serious discussion about the bodies in which we live. We all complain about our figures. I cannot remember ever meeting anyone who was completely satisfied with the way she looked. Without going through a complete makeover, there is some magic we can perform to improve not only the image we project to others but also our self-image. This improvement can give us confidence and direction in our design choices.

Do you know the proper clothing to wear to do the most for what you've got? Do you know what clothing to choose to look taller or shorter, thinner or rounder? Take a long, hard look at yourself in a full-length mirror, and let's go to work.

Your clothing can create the desired illusion if you know how to choose the right lines, colors, fabrics and silhouettes.

It's easy to draw attention to your assets, if you are honest enough with yourself to recognize the problem areas that should be disguised. Once you have this knowledge in your bag of tricks, you'll have no trouble maximizing each asset. You will present a "best self" to the world and take pleasure in your best self-image.

A narrow silhouette can make one appear smaller and slimmer while a full silhouette enlarges the form (figs. 3 and 4). To do the most for yourself, learn which silhouettes are the most favorable to you. For example, if you are average in build and height and want to look very tall and slim, reach for that long-line jacket and wear a skirt that is a little longer than usual (fig. 4). This will achieve the "model look." Or, if you have slim, square shoulders and wide hips (fig. 5) accent your shoulder line with a shape that fits smoothly. Downplay the hips by wearing a garment that flares gently from below the shoulders to the hemline, creating a modified tent shape or A-line silhouette.

Line is the stage setting for dressing and fashion

fig. 3　　　　　fig. 4　　　　　fig. 5

design. When we emphasize a feature with line, we attract the eye to that area and subordinate the rest. This is the first step towards appearing "well put together." With line, we can create mood, shape and direction. Curved lines help create grace, movement and femininity. Lines follow the general shape of the body and suggest softness (fig. 6).

Straight lines are the architectural lines. When they are horizontal, straight lines move the eye across the body, shortening the height and, at times, adding width (fig. 7). By careful placement of these horizontals, you can shorten your figure without widening it. A tunic is that type of garment. The eye is drawn down towards the hem, creating a slender illusion. An Empire line, on the other hand, raises the eye to the bosom, shortening an overly long neck or upper torso (fig. 8).

fig. 6   fig. 7   fig. 8

11

Vertical lines create the illusion of slender height. The eye will follow the dominant vertical, creating this illusion of height that most shorter women crave (fig. 9).

Diagonals move the eye both horizontally and vertically. If they are more vertical, diagonals will be slenderizing (fig. 10); when diagonals are more horizontal, the illusion will be wider (fig. 11). Diagonals seem to come and go on the fashion scene.

fig. 9

fig. 10

fig. 11

They are effective lines and can be personal statements because they are not as commonly used. Maybe this line loses commercial favor because it takes more fabric and effort to use it well.

We must also consider the *space* that lines create.

Spaces also direct the movement of the eye. For example, a wide front panel of a princess-line dress can actually make you look wider in spite of the vertical seaming (fig. 12). A narrow front panel will emphasize the vertical lines of the style (fig. 13).

fig. 12

fig. 13

Color

Color is the final element to be considered with space and line. Warm colors enlarge while cool colors diminish. That doesn't mean that a larger-sized woman should not wear red but she should use color wisely. If your frame is large, choose a red with blue in it to reduce the broadening effect. A very thin person selecting navy blue or black should consider a shiny fabric or bright shade of those colors to magnify her size.

Most of us have personal color preferences and we cling to those boundaries. Occasionally, we break away and add some fun things to our wardrobes that are in colors we don't normally choose. Such change injects new life into tired attitudes towards ourselves and our wardrobes. Our physical tones of skin, hair and eyes are based on colors of the spectrum. These colors predetermine our color range. We build it into our wardrobes, homes and everything we gather about us. Even though we often say we want to change the scheme of things, we usually end up coming right back to that basic theme. Don't fight with yourself—wear what your being dictates. Add an occasional zinger by way of these colors you "always wanted to try." The simplest way to incorporate them is to accessorize in some new mode to give yourself a fresh feeling towards your entire wardrobe. If you're having problems arriving at a personal color scheme, make an appointment with a qualified color consultant. You can find them listed in your local Yellow Pages. There's nothing like professional help for problem solving.

Fabrics

Fabric textures influence the final appearance and eye appeal of your clothing. Soft, clinging fabric is probably the most slenderizing, because it readily conforms to the body (fig. 14). This is great for slender people with wonderful figures. Clingy fabrics often reveal too many of our otherwise hidden figure faults (fig. 15). A firmer, lightweight fabric will minimize size while actually hiding some of our less desirable features. It will not lie so close and flat against the body.

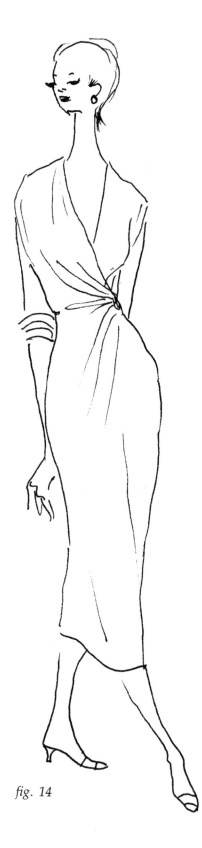

fig. 14

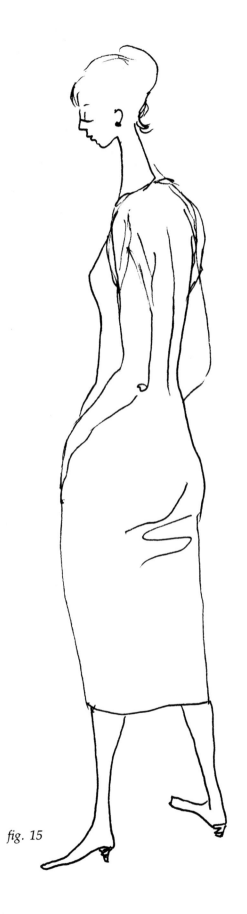

There are even some people in this world who feel that they are too thin. Crisp, lightweight fabrics give the ultra-slender group the appearance of more body weight in the warm weather. Heavy tweeds, highly textured woollens and fur fabrics produce bulk for your winter look.

Sheers can be worn by slender as well as generously proportioned women. These fabrics have no real size category, but they do reveal the shape underneath. Drape that fabric over your body at the shop before you make your purchases, for a sneak preview of how it will look in final form.

While on the subject of fabrics, I would like to include a standard list of symbols for fabric care. Too often we buy some fabric yardage with a tag of instructions that is nothing more than a triangle with a number inside—with no explanation of the symbol's meaning. I've even tried calling fabric shops for the answer and received several different responses about the same marking. Here's the universal mill coding list that should solve your fabric-care questions.

fig. 15

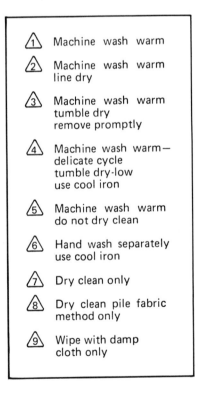

1. Machine wash warm
2. Machine wash warm line dry
3. Machine wash warm tumble dry remove promptly
4. Machine wash warm— delicate cycle tumble dry-low use cool iron
5. Machine wash warm do not dry clean
6. Hand wash separately use cool iron
7. Dry clean only
8. Dry clean pile fabric method only
9. Wipe with damp cloth only

Figure Types

Most of us pay little attention to the specifics of figure types. We blithely wend our way by trial and error, sewing, ripping out and discarding clothing, rarely realizing why that pattern looked so good on a neighbor and was a disaster on us. Now that you are drafting your own patterns you will probably be doing more sewing than ever before. Make it as rewarding and enjoyable, as you possibly can by knowing more about yourself. Study the information that applies to your figure type.

SHORT AND SLIM

Your figure is rather simple to deal with as you fall into an "ideal" category. If you want to achieve a tall, slim look (fig. 16), you should rely on vertical lines, both in the style and fabric. A well-proportioned shirtwaist dress of lightweight fabric, yoked garments and tent-shaped dresses will certainly add to your stature. Blouson styling is also for you *if* you stay within your scale of proportions. Avoid dresses with undefined shapes, such as loose-fitting shifts; they can make you appear shorter and much too boxy. Concentrate on an uncluttered appearance

fig. 16

fig. 17

that is proportioned to your height. Unnecessary bulk from wide, swirling skirts or heavy fabrics should be avoided in favor of short, well-fitted jackets, gently flaring skirts and more delicate details (fig. 17). Shape your clothing with gathers, shirring or vertical tucks; these details produce vertical lines. If pleats are stitched down to the hipline, this, too, adds to the illusion of height. Warm colors, lightweight and smooth fabrics, and shiny finishes are important for your wardrobe. Shun large prints; you don't want your clothes to wear *you* (fig. 18). Small prints and subtle patterns will be flattering; but avoid overpowering styles and details. Strong horizontal bands considerably shorten your stature. Stay with a monochromatic color plan. Select lightweight, lightly textured fabrics for the most mileage from your new wardrobe.

When choosing pants, go for straight-leg slacks or jeans. These will give you the tallest look (fig. 19). You can also wear pants that are slightly flared at the bottom; this line has a very upward movement. A tunic or blouse, hip-length jacket or a hip-length or short vest would make good toppers. You can also wear shorts of any length, knickers (plus fours), gauchos, culottes and slim, fitted jumpsuits.

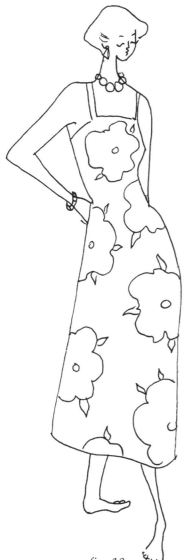

fig. 18

fig. 19

SHORT AND HEAVY

You are not only seeking height, but also slenderizing lines. A-line, asymmetric styles and princess lines are your prime choices. Surplice dresses diagonally overlapping in front, can be very flattering (fig. 20). Vertical lines should be dominant in your wardrobe, including subtle patterns and vertical stripes. Freely use pleats—stitched and unstitched—prominent vertical seaming and other vertical detailing. V-necklines are perfect for you. Avoid large, bold prints and horizontal lines, such as wide belts in contrasting colors, or very short skirts. These carry the eye across the body rather than up and down and can easily make you look like you're wearing the box the fabric came in! Empire styles, low waistlines and strongly defined yokes will only widen and shorten your silhouette. They are a real "no-no." Avoid clingy styles and fabrics because they reveal figure flaws. Don't over-accessorize, as a cluttered look can be easily achieved in a small area. Choose fabrics with flat finishes. Avoid color extremes and shiny finishes.

Straight-legged pants with a matching tunic will give you a long, slim look (fig. 21). Your variations could be jumpsuits, culottes (in all lengths) or gauchos (but not too full). Avoid shorts; they tend to widen the figure.

fig. 20

fig. 21

TALL AND SLIM

Yours is the figure "in the catbird seat," the figure that can wear anything, the model figure. A-line, blouson, shirtwaist or the huge, 1980s oversized look—they're all your "bowl of cherries." You can wear stripes, plaids, prints and highly textured fabrics and look right. You're limited only by personal choice (fig. 22).

Every variety of pants will look good on you—short shorts to widely flared palazzo pants. You can even top these with a selection of bulky tops or oversized sweaters. For you, the sky's the limit.

TALL AND HEAVY

Easy-fitting clothing with vertical or diagonal lines should dominate your wardrobe. Vests and long cardigans are very becoming but not boleros or Eton jackets. The latter two styles tend to draw the eye horizontally instead of vertically (fig. 23). Avoid patterns at both ends of the size scale. Extremes will not flatter you. For your accessories, observe a proper scale, such as purses that won't get lost in your hand.

Wear cooler shades and greyed tones that flatter the face. Flat fabrics with subtle surface treatment

fig. 22

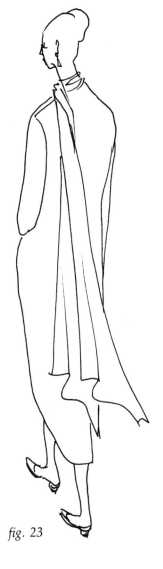

fig. 23

should be your direction. Avoid clingy fabrics that can reveal what you're trying to disguise. Choose straight-leg pants rather than capri pants that taper sharply from the top of the leg to the ankle. Don't wear them tight enough to display figure faults that are better hidden. A tunic or vest would top your pants nicely. You might even try culottes, palazzos or gauchos (fig. 24). Any of these styles are becoming to you.

TOP-HEAVY

Easy-fitting shirts, blouson styling and low-waisted dresses with interest at the hip or hemline should be your choices (fig. 25). Avoid capes, Empire styles and yoked bodices. Details should be below the waist, rather than above, to draw the eye down to your asset—your slender hips. Avoid snug-fitting or very short tops, fluffy collars and too-short

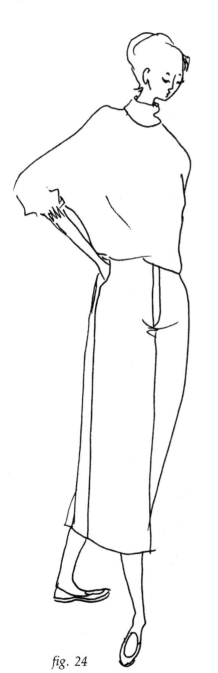

fig. 24

fig. 25

sleeves; in other words, styling that attracts too much attention to the bosom or shoulder areas. Favor darker colors for your bodice with lighter or patterned skirts. Hipline belts will flatter your figure as will contrasting banding at the lower portion of the dress.

Choose pants with a slight flare or soft, straight trousers to balance your upper and lower proportions. Top these with a hip-length vest (jerkin) to minimize your problem. Knickers and long culottes are flattering styles for you (fig. 26).

HIP-HEAVY

Tent-shaped dresses were designed with your figure in mind (fig. 27). Vertical lines that lead the eye to your face and neckline are your best options. Avoid the sheath dress; it will only accent your hips. Skirts shaped with darts or gores, A-line or wrap skirts will even up your look. Avoid horizontal bands across the hips, overblouses that don't cover your hipline and little Peter Pan collars. Combinations of the above details tend to make your figure

fig. 26   fig. 27

appear somewhat pear-shaped. A light-colored bodice with a dark skirt is a great combination for you. Be sure to match the belt to the skirt.

You would probably do better in loose-fitting, rather than straight-legged, pants. Culottes, gauchos and palazzo pants are graceful styles for your wardrobe (fig. 28). An easy-fitting tunic or jacket that covers the fullest part of your hip could be a little lighter in color to draw the eye upwards, creating a slimmer appearance.

fig. 28

HALF-SIZE AND QUEEN-SIZE

Easy-fitting garments with particular emphasis on vertical lines are your best directions. Opt for solid colors and avoid bold prints and bulky fabrics. Choose clothes that are proportioned for your generous figure, but don't sacrifice style. Your pattern-drafting talents can put new and exciting ideas into a suitable perspective for your figure.

Follow your innate taste, consider the proportion of your silhouette and enjoy your decisions. These are the garments *you* will be wearing. There's never been a better time in fashion to express yourself.

Remember that queen-size or half-size denotes a figure type, not your age. Queen-size shops have popped up all over the country catering to very young teens and matrons as well as to more mature women who cannot otherwise be fitted for clothing. The styles are designed and produced by the finest, most advanced fashion houses in the world, which are finally catering to your figure problems.

These wonderful designs are also spilling over into the pattern books. If you're a teenager and need a half-size, you no longer have to wear clothes that look like grandma's hand-me-downs. All the latest styles are now available to you. The only consideration you have is the same as anyone else's: your figure type. You may need a half-size or queen-size, but are you top-heavy or hip-heavy? Are you tall or short? Then look up in this book the category that defines your figure and read about your figure type. Seek out the queen-size dealers in your area. Try on some of the new garments that have been designed with your figure problems in mind, and when you're ready to sew for yourself, keep those styles in mind. Your relative's or a friend's dress or blouse can be used as a basis for your pattern. If you're not a teenager any more but just love fashion, whether it be high style or funky, you too, will be very pleased to find that there are *fashion* ideas available to you.

Compare the costs of sewing to buying a similar garment. Sometimes, buying a "sale" garment can be cheaper than sewing it, and it also provides you with an item you'll love to wear. It can be used as a sloper (basic pattern), influencing your wardrobe for years to come. You will no longer be wondering what to sew or how garments will look on you when they're completed. Armed with personal fashion knowledge, you can make sewing a joy.

DRAFTING
PATTERNS

fig. 29

CLOTHES WITH CAPPED SLEEVES

The information detailed in this chapter is the key to the entire concept of drafting patterns from finished clothes. Study the concept and practical application carefully, as everything you will be doing is based on the contents of these pages. Each page was designed to lead you through the learning process step by step. Reading the information will familiarize you with the method, but there is no substitute for trying this system yourself. Producing a garment from *your* personal pattern that you can wear and enjoy will integrate this technique into your permanent sewing skills.

When you are thoroughly familiar with the method and are ready to draft your first pattern, choose a style as simple as the one I describe below. It will make the pattern-drafting system much easier to absorb.

Choosing a Garment

I have an elegant knit tunic with a drawstring waistline and cowl collar that I enjoy wearing with slacks and jeans. It is so comfortable that I find myself living in it, wishing that I had a pattern to make a dress—*the dress*—that perfect go-everywhere, do-everything dress that we always seek. I will use this tunic to demonstrate the method of drafting a simple pattern for such a desired dress (fig. 29).

SURVEY: CLOTHES WITH CAPPED SLEEVES

Before you begin drafting a pattern, there are questions about any garment that should be answered.

You should be familiar with the style, cut and all details of the item. Study Survey Questions (below) to familiarize yourself with the garment you've chosen, and pinpoint the information you need to draft your pattern.

Survey Questions: Clothes with Capped Sleeves

1. Is the garment cut on the lengthwise grain (parallel to the selvage) or on the bias (diagonal)?

2. What is the style of the sleeves? How are they set?

3. Are there any style or size changes that I want to make as I draft my pattern?

4. Is the length correct?

5. Will my version be of similar fabric, or must I add additional inches for ease?

6. Are there any parts of this garment that are cut from straight pieces of fabric where I might note the measurements instead of making an additional pattern piece?

A survey of my tunic revealed the following information:

- *Collar:* Full cowl cut from one lengthwise piece of fabric.

- *Sleeves:* Simple caps, extensions of the shoulder line.

- *Body:* Straight line from the underarm down to the hemline.

- *Waistline:* Casing for drawstring stitched around the tunic waistline.

- *Pockets:* Inseam pockets at each side.
- *Fabric:* Horizontally striped cotton knit. Stripes will simplify matching the pattern lines and other construction details.

My fabric hoard in the sewing room disclosed a beautiful piece of raw silk that draped as softly as a knit and measured 60 inches (152.4 cm) in width. I was fully aware that it was a woven fabric, not a knit like the original tunic. I knew this soft raw silk could be substituted for the original knit. Additional ease was not necessary because the tunic was very full. As the raw silk was unusually wide I figured that I could easily cut the *front* and *back* by placing the patterns side by side across the fabric width (fig. 30). One selvage side could be used for the drawstring, and the casing could be cut from the opposite side. The pockets could come out of the center scrap. Perfect! I had already decided not to put a collar on this dress. A simple boat neckline would be a far better foil for my jewelry. (I noted the collar size for future use.) Now, let's make the pattern so that it can be reused as many times as desired.

DETERMINING SEAM WIDTH

Commercial patterns have a ⅝-inch (16-mm) seam allowance to provide enough fabric for individual figure adjustments. When you draft your own pattern from a garment you have already worn, you know exactly how it fits you and are aware of any needed adjustments. In other words, when you cut additional garments from your own patterns or from garments you have worn and enjoyed, you know those new garments will fit perfectly each time. Since you have no need for adjustment you have no need for large seams that produce excess bulk inside the garment.

I use a ¼-inch (6-mm) seam allowance when drafting patterns. This seam will lie flat and is a perfect width for a serging stitch that closes the seam and overcasts in one operation. If you prefer another type of seam finishing, allow ½ inch (13 mm) on all seams. This is a more than ample seam allowance and will still lie flat.

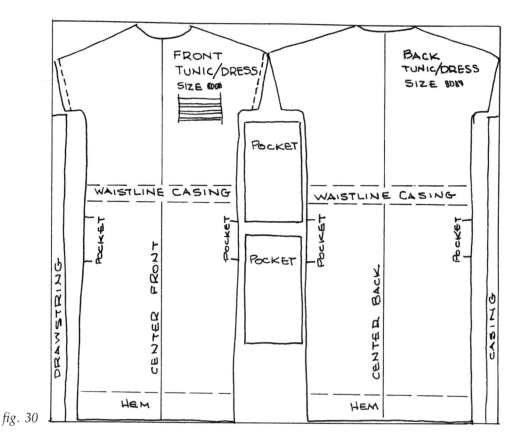

fig. 30

PREPARING PATTERN PAPER

If the pattern paper you have chosen is not large enough to completely cover the garment, tape two or three pieces together to form a sheet *larger* than the garment.

Back

Lay the pattern paper on your cutting table or other large, flat surface. Place the garment *back* down on the sheet with the shoulders equidistant from the top of the page. Smooth out any wrinkles in the garment and be sure the pattern paper is visible on all sides (fig. 31). With this method, you draft a pattern piece of the complete front and back each time: front (left and right); back (left and right). Drafting a *complete* pattern rather than a half means that you'll never have to go back and draw the other half to use it with special fabrics. Especially when cutting plaid, patterned fabric or leather, a complete pattern is a must. These fabrics should never be cut on the fold. With a complete front and back pattern, all patterns are ready to use.

STEP 1

Beginning at the neck edge of one shoulder, draw short dashes or dots around your garment, approximately ¼ inch (6 mm) outside the outer edge. These markings suggest an outline that will become your cutting line (fig. 32). Be sure you have included your chosen seam allowance as you draw.

DRAFTING DETAILS

The cap sleeve of this sample tunic is a continuation of the shoulder line. Draw the line out to the end of the cap and add 1 inch (2.5 cm) hem allowance at the bottom. Indicate the waistline with a horizontal dash (see markings on fig. 32). Make a mark in the side seam allowance for the placement of the in-seam pockets. Also, mark the length of the existing garment (plus the hem allowance). This is the information needed to repeat the tunic. Since we are drafting a dress pattern use a tape measure or yardstick to measure from your waistline to your skirt length. Add approximately 2 inches (5.1 cm) for the hem allowance along the bottom of the new dress (fig. 32).

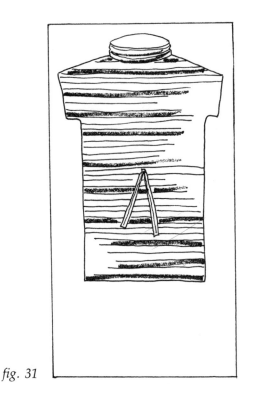

fig. 31

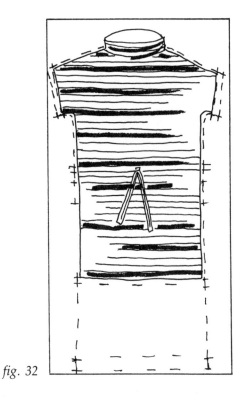

fig. 32

When you have marked around the garment, indicated the hemlines, lower edges, pocket placements and waistline, carefully fold your garment in half lengthwise. Mark the center or lowest point at the back of the neck (fig. 33). Rough-in the curve of this opening, starting from the marked point where the shoulder and neck edges meet. Follow the curve down to the lowest point or *center back* that you just marked on the pattern and continue up to the point where the neckline curve meets the beginning of the opposite shoulder line. Mark this point. Remove the garment from the paper. You now have a rough outline of the *back*—your first pattern.

STEP 2

Matching the shoulders and side seams of your rough draft as closely as possible, fold the paper lengthwise. Reopen the sheet and draw this line down the center of the pattern piece with your contrasting pen and yardstick (fig. 34). This is the lengthwise grain, *center back* or *on-fold* line for cutting plain fabrics.

If a solid fabric crawls slightly in the cutting there is no real problem. But a plaid must be carefully matched, not only from side to side but also from back to front. Therefore, plaids should be cut from the opened fabric. This is why I stress the drafting of the entire pattern piece: left and right halves of the *front* and *back*. It is far more practical to line up matching points and cut a garment from a completed pattern piece, than to move a pattern half (as necessary with commercial pattern pieces) and take chances on possible errors that could cost you the entire fabric. This eliminates a potential pitfall. The finished results will be all the proof you need.

Refold your paper on the center line and compare the two halves. At several points down the length of the center line, measure out to each of the side edges to be certain that both sides are identical. Correct any marks that are out of line. There is another way to be sure both sides of a pattern piece will match: refold the paper on the center line and hold it up against the light (a window in daylight or a lamp). The light shines through both sides of the paper. Then, you can check to be sure that all mark-

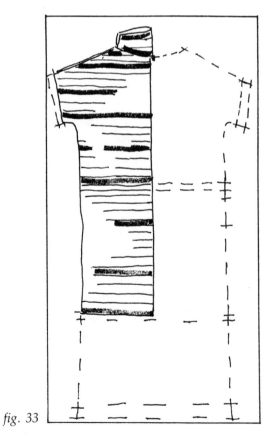

fig. 33

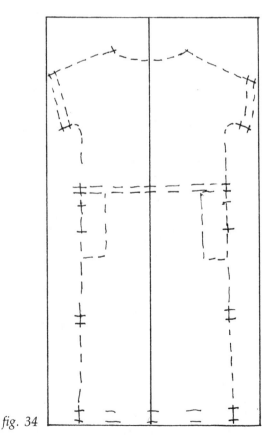

fig. 34

ings are visually aligned. Correct any marks that appear to be off. Reopen the paper and lay it back on the table.

FINALIZING THE OUTLINE

Now take the contrasting pen and yardstick and connect all the short marks you made to outline the garment. The contrasting pen will make the solid lines far more visible in the midst of the original dashes or dots with which you roughed-in your outline (fig. 35).

Draw a double line to connect the markings you made for the waistline. This is the placement for the drawstring casing. Draw another solid horizontal line to indicate the bottom edge of the tunic, the hem of the tunic, the lower edge (dress length) and the line of the 2-inch (5.1-cm) hem allowance. On the side seams (within the proper marks) note the pocket placement. Be sure to identify the purpose of each line as you finalize it.

CODING THE PATTERNS

Your personal patterns should be fully identified for future use. You will have all these important details if they are carefully listed on the patterns when you draft them. A simple method for coding is:

- Your size and weight at the time your pattern is drafted (one's weight does fluctuate).

- Current date (this gives you a pattern number for cataloguing).

- Type of garment: *tunic/dress* (*back*) (fig. 36).

This method of labelling (or any other system that you find convenient) should be used for every pattern piece that you draft. The alternative—guesswork—can result in some strange garments.

The first section of the pattern—the *back*—is now complete. Set it aside and prepare another sheet of pattern paper to draft the *front* pattern.

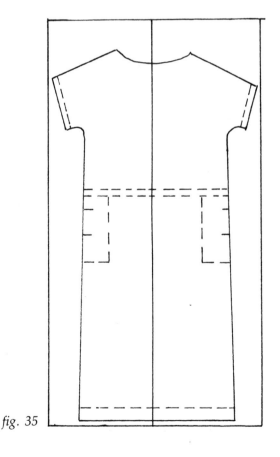

fig. 35

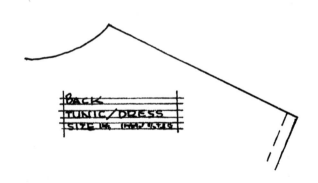

fig. 36

Front

When I surveyed this tunic I found that the front was a little wider than the *back* to allow for that lovely draping. Adding a little extra to the front allows the garment to drape without looking too big. To draft the pattern, lay the garment *front* down on the paper to let the excess fabric roll to the top. An equal amount of fabric must be added to each side of this pattern piece to achieve a balanced drape (fig. 37). When sketching the *front*, I was very careful to maintain this excess just as I saw it on the original garment.

Very detailed information was supplied to complete the *back* pattern. Follow this simple checklist and same method for the *front*. If you have doubts about the drafting method, refer back to the section on the *back* pattern (page 27).

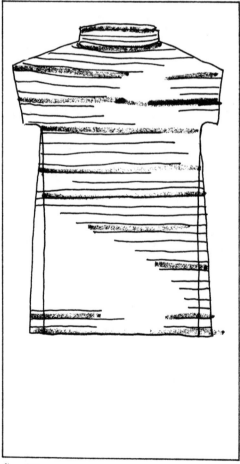

fig. 37

Checklist: Simple Garments

1. Draw dashes or dots completely around the garment.

2. Indicate the lowest or center point of the neck opening.

3. Find the center line of the pattern piece.

4. Draw in the neckline.

5. Check all the markings by measuring out from the center line or refolding the pattern piece and comparing the two halves.

6. Finish all lines with contrasting pen and yardstick.

7. Detail all necessary information on the pattern piece: date, type of garment, and re-designed style. (Don't forget to label the piece *front* or *back*.)

8. Identify all markings: waistline, hems, pocket placements and any unusual details.

9. Completely detail any necessary sewing instructions.

10. Add current size: weight or measurements.

CONSTRUCTION

I eliminated the pockets from this dress, because I thought the texture of the raw silk might cause them to curl inside the dress. Since I usually prefer pockets, I carefully noted their size and shape on my pattern for future use. Inseam pocket information is detailed on page 32.

Following is an outline of the sewing details for this dress.

1. Make an eyelet or buttonhole at the marked point on the *center front* that will be large enough to admit the drawstring (fig. 38). This should be done *before* the sections of the garment are sewn together, as there is less fabric to handle.

2. If pockets are included, they will be inserted at this point (see Inseam Pockets below).

3. Sew shoulder seams and side seams (fig. 39).

4. Stitch the drawstring casing to the dress along the designated line (fig. 40).

5. Make the drawstring and cut it at the center. Add 2 to 3 inches (5.1 to 7.6 cm) of elastic (approximately the same width as the drawstring) to the center (fig. 41). This makes the string fit securely without feeling tight. Thread it through the casing with a large safety pin.

6. After cutting the garment, there wasn't enough fabric left to make a facing for the neckline. I substituted lace seam binding and topstitched around the neck opening.

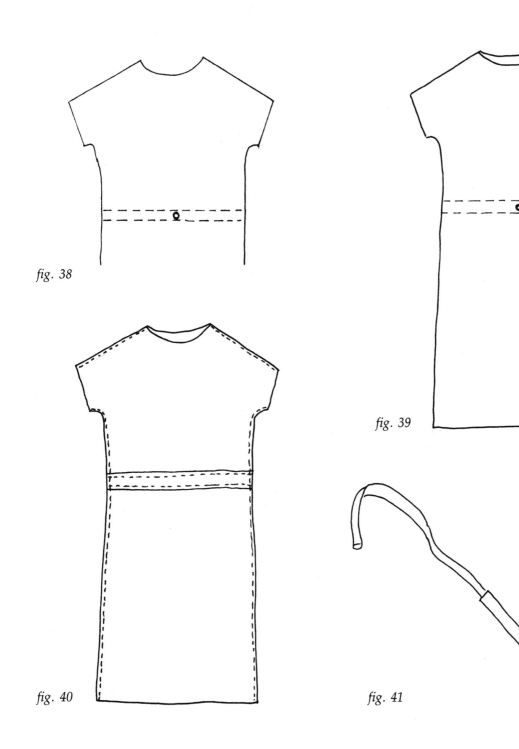

fig. 38

fig. 39

fig. 40

fig. 41

The dress is now ready for hemming. Lace seam tape makes a nice finish for the hem edge and will pass easily through the needle bed when blind-hemming on your sewing machine. It also handles well when hand-hemming (fig. 42).

fig. 42

Inseam Pockets

Following is the method that I find easiest for inserting pockets. It is a part of the total construction of the garment.

1. Cut two pieces of fabric, each 10 by 12 inches (25.4 by 30.5 cm), from a scrap of matching dress fabric. These will become your pockets (fig. 43).

2. Place the pockets on the *front* of the dress with the right sides of the fabric together. The top edge (10-inch [25.4-cm] side) should overlap the waistline with the 12-inch (30.5-cm) side parallel to the side seam. Sew along the **X**s to within 2 inches (5.1 cm) of the bottom edge of the pocket (fig. 44).

3. Open pockets out, away from the garment (fig. 45).

4. Put *back* and *front* together with right sides facing each other. Align the unsewn edge of the pocket with the pocket markings of the *back*. Pin the top edge to the waistline markings. Sew the edge of the pocket to the *back* along the **X**s. Repeat for opposite pocket (fig. 46).

5. With right sides of the dress together, the pockets will fold in half vertically. Stitch the outside seam from the hem to the bottom of the pocket. Continue stitching approximately 2 inches (5.1 cm) beyond the point where the stitching crosses the bottom edge of the pocket. Reverse the dress and stitch a curved line from that point down to the lower edge of the pocket (fig. 47). You may either continue to stitch along the folded edge or break off and begin again at the waistline. Continue to the end of the sleeve. Stitch the shoulder seams and complete the opposite side (fig. 47).

6. If your garment calls for a drawstring casing, sew it to the garment at this point, catching the pocket tops into the lower line of stitching. If your garment calls for a waistband, catch the pocket tops into the seam as it is stitched (fig. 48).

7. Turn the garment right side out. Stitch-in-the-ditch (in the slot of the seam) for approximately 2 inches (5.1 cm) down from the lower edge of the casing. Skip 4½ to 5 inches (11.4 to 12.7 cm) for

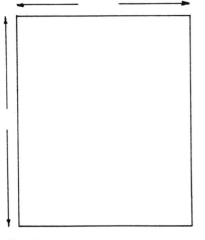

fig. 43

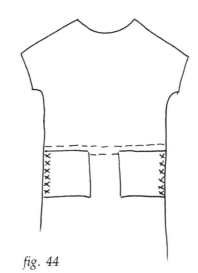

fig. 44

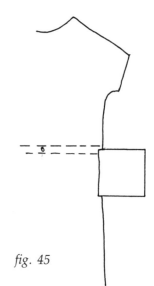

fig. 45

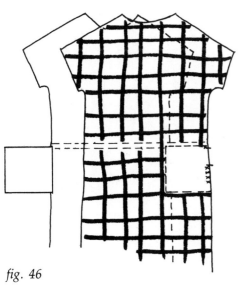

fig. 46

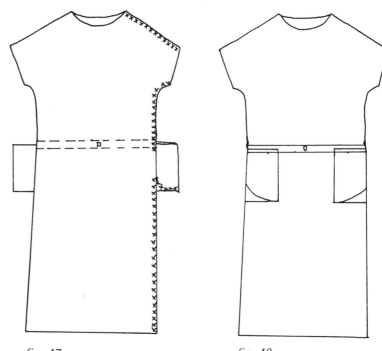

fig. 47

fig. 48

the pocket opening and then stitch to the bottom of the pocket. Repeat on the opposite side (fig. 49). This method will usually keep your pockets from rolling inside the garment.

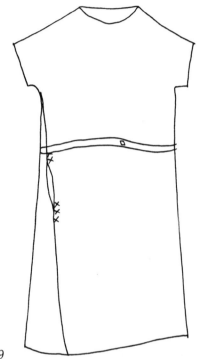

fig. 49

GENERAL INFORMATION

When I first started drafting my own patterns, I began noting as many details as possible directly on one of the major pattern pieces thereby eliminating the loss potential. All small, straight pattern pieces and measurements are sketched and detailed on either the *front* or the *back* of the pattern. That is why I have not mentioned pattern pieces for the cowl collar, drawstring or casing. During the original survey, it was determined that these three pieces were cut from straight pieces of fabric. We will not make a separate pattern for these pieces. Carefully measure each one and note these measurements directly on the pattern. They'll never wander off again.

Detail all instructions for cutting, etc., in the same manner, and you won't ever have to wonder what became of your direction sheets, either. Remember, you will be using this pattern again in the future.

Using Your Pattern Creatively

Changing or redesigning a pattern isn't limited to turning a simple tunic into a street-length dress. The original tunic would adapt beautifully to anything from active sportswear to evening clothes.

Instead of stopping the hemline at street length, why not lower it to ankle length (fig. 50)? If the

fig. 50

width of your skirt seems too narrow for a floor-length dress, you can create additional width by swinging the pattern (widening the angle from the center line). This isn't as complicated as it sounds. Just lay out the pattern in the usual manner (fig. 51) and cut the shoulder line and sleeve extension (fig. 52). The pattern is then swung off-center approximately 2 inches (5.1 cm) at the lower edge (fig. 53). This will give the dress an A-line effect and create ample walking room. The longer skirt is a part of the "lean" look, and you can be comfortable when wearing it.

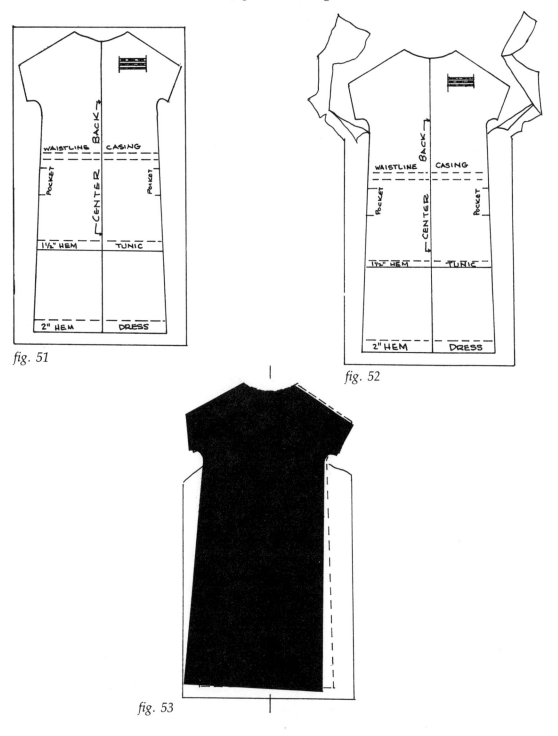

fig. 51

fig. 52

fig. 53

Interpreting these patterns into completely new garments puts the fun back into sewing. If you enjoy wearing sweat shirts, try the ideas on the following pages using your basic pattern. First, make some thumbnail sketches of changes you can make to give your pattern a whole new look—neckline changes, different types of pockets, belt and waistband treatments. Try some ideas on the finished garment before you start cutting a new one from the same pattern. Scarves can be draped around your shoulders to suggest new neckline shapes. Belts might inspire waistline variations (fig.

fig. 54

54). Measure the distance from the waistline to the floor to determine the length you will need for a long style. Make a note of the floor length, shinbone length and ankle length, because you will probably be using these figures again. Lay the pattern directly on the fabric, leaving enough additional fabric at the bottom to accommodate the new length you've chosen. There is no need to cut a new pattern to make these changes in dress length.

A **kimono sleeve** is a natural extension of the tunic's capped sleeve and is merely a rectangular piece of fabric folded on the lengthwise grain. It is as wide as the lower edge of the sleeve, plus seam allowance. The length of a kimono sleeve is the distance between the bottom edge of the original cap sleeve and your wristbone, plus hem allowance. Measure the amount of fabric you will need for each sleeve directly on the fabric (fig. 55).

Stitch to the sleeve edge after the shoulder seam is completed and before the side seams are closed.

Inseam, patch or kangaroo pockets are a great addition to this design. Make a cozy **at-home robe** with hand-warmers for those chilly evenings (fig. 56).

fig. 55

fig. 56

Putting these garments together is really quite simple. The first step is sewing the pockets to the open fabric. Stitch shoulder seams together and then open out the garment. Stitch the new sleeve additions to the edge of the cap. Then you can stitch the side seams in one continuous line from the hemline to the end of the sleeve.

The sleeve edge can be finished in several ways.

1. Fold up the hem allowance and finish with one or more rows of top stitching or machine embroidery. (Hemming can also be done in the more conventional manners.)

2. Create a casing at the lower edge of the sleeve and insert narrow elastic.

3. Add bias strips of a contrasting color to bind off. With right sides of the fabric together, stitch the binding to the edges of the sleeve, turn under and then stitch-in-the-ditch. These facings can be stitched in the opposite direction so that the trim can be turned to the outside for contrast and stitched.

The hem can be done using the same methods as number 1 or 3 above. Another way to finish your lounger is to create slits at one or both sides of the garment and either finish as suggested above or make a facing by cutting two strips of matching or contrasting fabric (fig. 57). These should be the length of the slit (including hem allowance) plus 2 inches (5.1 cm) for securing it at the top, by 2 to 3 inches (5.1 to 7.6 cm) width. Then, stitch the facing at the cut edges of the slit, from the hem to the upper edge of the opening. To finish, either slip-stitch by hand or machine-stitch at the edges. For a more interesting detail, use contrasting fabric for the facings. Attach them so they will fold to the outside of the garment instead of underneath and topstitch them in place. Nice detail!

More Ideas

This, or any other simple pattern lends itself beautifully to terry cloth. The original pattern could be

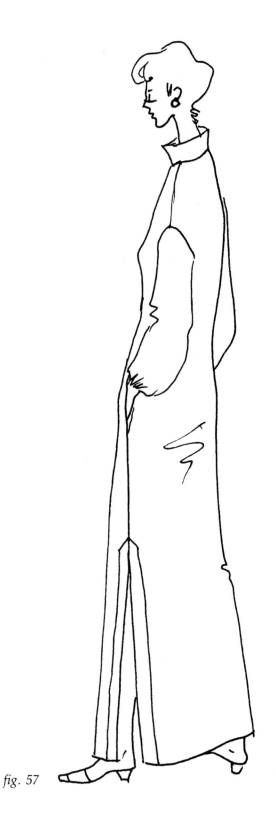

fig. 57

varied by cutting a **shirttail hemline** (fig. 58). After all, hems don't always have to be cut straight across.

You may also try this pattern using cotton knit or printed nylon for a very comfortable **nightgown** (fig. 59). Use narrow lingerie elastic in the waistline casing. Or for a more feminine look, use lace edging around the neckline, sleeves and/or the bottom (fig. 60).

fig. 58

fig. 59

For warding off the winter chill make this gown using flannel. You could turn up a ½-inch hem (13-mm) and topstitch it on your machine with one of the embroidery stitches (fig. 61). Create it in several lengths: baby doll, street, waltz or floor length; the pattern will look new each time. For a different look, try a V-neckline (fig. 62). When you do try some of these variations, keep careful notes to repeat these tricks with different fabrics. Instead of the inseam pockets, add two big patch pockets and bind them with ribbon or contrasting bias binding. Rather than finishing the hem straight across the bottom, try a

fig. 60   fig. 61   fig. 62

shirttail look—wonderful after a tub or shower (fig. 63). Eliminate the waistline casing and allow the garment to hang loose. It can always be belted if you're in the mood for a more fitted look.

The original tunic length of the garment we've been working with would be great in velour with matching **pull-on pants**. Omit the waistline casing and cut a shirttail hem. You might even want to add ribbing at the neckline, cuffs and/or pants hem . . . or maybe even a pouch pocket (fig. 64)?

fig. 63

fig. 64

If you are going to a dressy party and have nothing to wear, cut this pattern in satin or printed silk (fig. 65). A ruffle around the neckline or cascading down the front would be very pretty and feminine too—another easy trick. For a 2-inch (5.1-cm)-wide ruffle, you need one and one half to two times the distance to be covered. For a very wide ruffle, cut the fabric on the bias; it will hang better. The simplicity of this dress lends itself to almost any skirt length.

Velour is a wonderful fabric for **at-home clothing** and would make up into great lounge dresses from this pattern—not only comfortable but very easy to care for. Add kimono sleeves and the cowl collar. Be sure you include the pockets for at-home wear. It's always nice to have a place to store your hanky. Give some thought to adding a hood to any of these garments (fig. 66). Not just a glamorous addition, the hood has a practical side, too—great for draping over just-washed hair or closing out a sudden draft on winter nights.

Be inventive. Put the fun back into your sewing.

Before you go on to the second project, *use* all of the information diagrammed in the first chapter. Follow the directions as they are laid out without skipping any pages or sections, because the points that are fully detailed in the first chapter of this book will only be lightly touched on in the next chapter.

fig. 65

fig. 66

fig. 67

CLOTHES WITH SET-IN SLEEVES

Choosing a Garment

By creating the first pattern in the preceding chapter, you learned how easy pattern drafting can be. But all of the patterns you want to make won't be based on capped-sleeve garments of knitted fabrics. There are styles of woven fabric with shaped collars and sleeves that can become part of your personal pattern file. These collar and sleeve details obviously call for additional pattern pieces, but they do not change or complicate the pattern-drafting process—they merely extend it.

The same basic steps will be repeated for your second pattern—the long-sleeved shirt. This chapter includes the technique for handling the sleeves to expose the armhole opening and the curve of the sleeve cap where it joins the armhole.

When choosing a garment to draft your second pattern, try to keep it as simple as the one in the illustration (fig. 67). This type of shirt provides the necessary elements.

SURVEY: CLOTHES WITH SET-IN SLEEVES

Complete a survey for each new garment before starting the pattern to familiarize yourself with the details and construction of the garment and to ease the process of creating the pattern. Answer the Survey Questions that follow and jot down your analysis.

Survey Questions: Clothes with Set-in sleeves

1. What is the general shape of the garment: straight or fitted?

2. What is the style of the front: pull-on, zippered or buttoned? Is there a placket or hidden closure?

3. What is the sleeve style, and how are the sleeves set in?

4. What is the collar style: straight or curved?

5. Is the garment cut on the lengthwise grain or on the bias?

6. Do I need any size or style changes as the pattern is drafted?

7. Will my version be made from a similar fabric, or will I need additional ease?

8. Can any pattern pieces be eliminated by recording the dimensions on the sloper (your personal pattern)?

I surveyed the shirt illustrated in this chapter and listed the following information:

- *Style:* Simple shirt.

- *Collar:* Slightly curved; will need pattern piece.

- *Sleeves:* Set-in long sleeve; straight cuff.

- *Body:* Straight, no darts.

- *Front:* Short placket with 4 buttons.

- *Fabric:* Woven cotton; pattern can be used for other fabrics without any changes, because I like my clothes to fit easy.

PREPARING PATTERN PAPER

Prepare the pattern paper as described on page 27. Refer to the checklist on page 30 to refresh your memory on drafting the pattern for the body of the shirt. If you wish to use your finished pattern for a dress or robe either street length or floor length, leave enough paper at the bottom of the *front* and *back* to include the alternate lengths you have chosen plus the hem allowance.

Back

Place the garment *front* down on the paper with the shoulders equidistant from the top of the page. Roughly outline the body of the shirt. Pull the sleeves into the body of the garment to expose the complete armhole curve (fig. 68). Put your hand up through the garment and into the sleeve; grasp the cuff and pull the sleeve through, turning the sleeve inside out and exposing the armhole curve as completely as possible. Smooth out the sleeve; be sure it is lying flat with no ripples or pulls at the armhole opening. Any wrinkles on this line will distort the armhole opening of the final pattern.

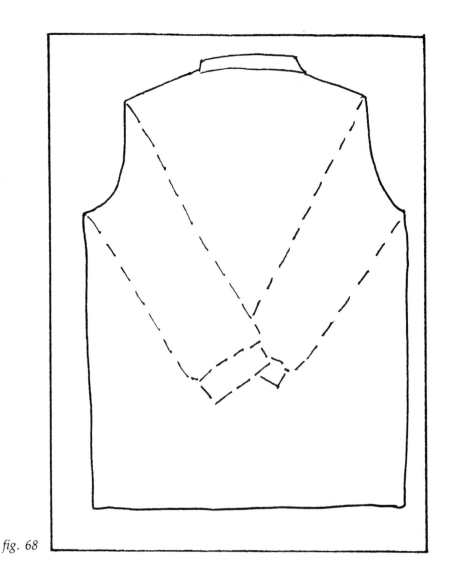

fig. 68

STEP 1

Starting at the neck edge of one shoulder, using a marker, rough-in the shoulder line and include the seam allowance. The line you sketch will become your cutting line. Mark the neck edge and outer point of the shoulder line with a perpendicular dash. Trace around the curve of the armhole opening and continue tracing down the side of the garment to the hem (fig. 69). Indicate the hem allowance along the bottom edge of the shirt. Complete the outline of the other half of the *back*.

STEP 2

Before you finalize the outlines, compare the armhole opening of your pattern with the armhole opening of a commercial pattern piece that you already have used and that fits comfortably. A cross-check of your pattern will prove that your outlines are correct and will give you confidence in your drawing.

STEP 3

When you have finalized the lines of the *back*, make all the necessary construction marks and sewing notes on the pattern piece.

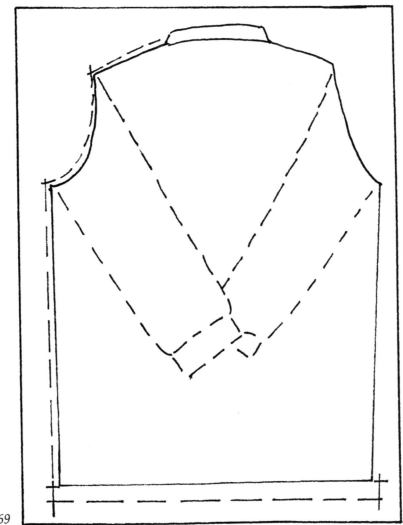

fig. 69

Front

Turn the shirt over on a new sheet of pattern paper (fig. 70) and complete the outline of the *front* as you did for the *back*. Refold the sleeves into the body of the garment (fig. 71). Suggest the outline of the armhole opening and complete this pattern piece (fig. 72). Again, cross-check the *front* armhole opening with a commercial pattern piece. Mark all construction details. Be sure to include your weight and/or measurements for future reference.

When all the marks are cross-checked and the lines finalized, write all details on the *front* and set the piece aside.

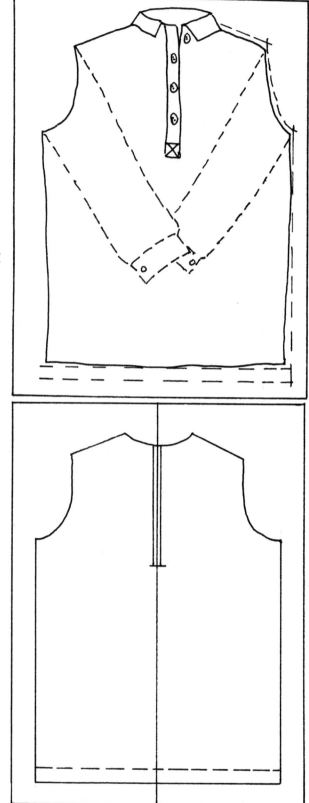

fig. 71

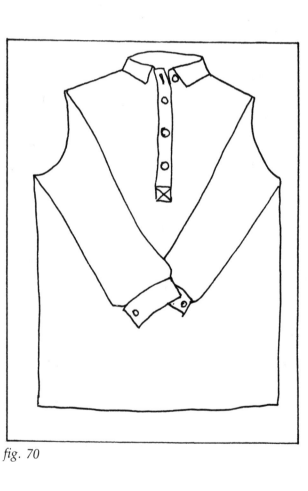

fig. 70

fig. 72

Sleeve

Prepare a sheet of pattern paper large enough to extend beyond the length of the sleeve and twice the width of the folded sleeve (fig. 73). Place the sleeve on the paper and spread it until the lower part of the sleeve lies flat. (The cap [sleeve top] will be slightly gathered where it was eased into the upper part of the armhole opening, but we will adjust for that later.) The center or folded edge of the sleeve should be at the approximate center of the paper with the underarm curve pointing towards the outer edge of the paper to allow enough room to draw the entire sleeve.

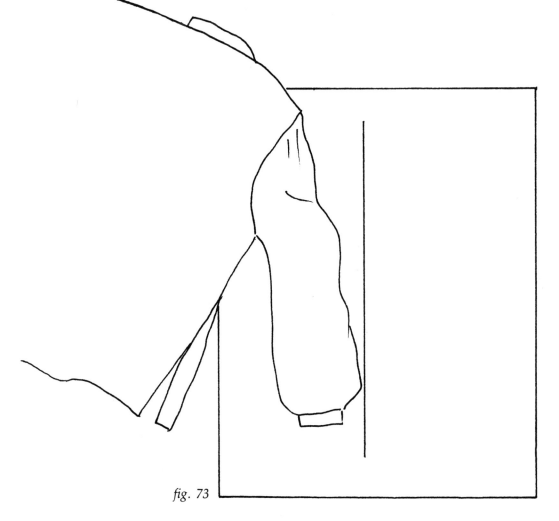

fig. 73

STEP 1

Start your dashes or dots down the underarm seam line from the armhole to the bottom edge of the sleeve. Indicate the bottom edge and hem allowance and carry both these lines across to the center point of the sleeve (fig. 74). Mark these points. Insert pins along the fold of the sleeve to identify the center. At the top where the center of the sleeve cap should meet the shoulder seam, make another mark. This is the correction for the take-up or ease of the stitched sleeve.

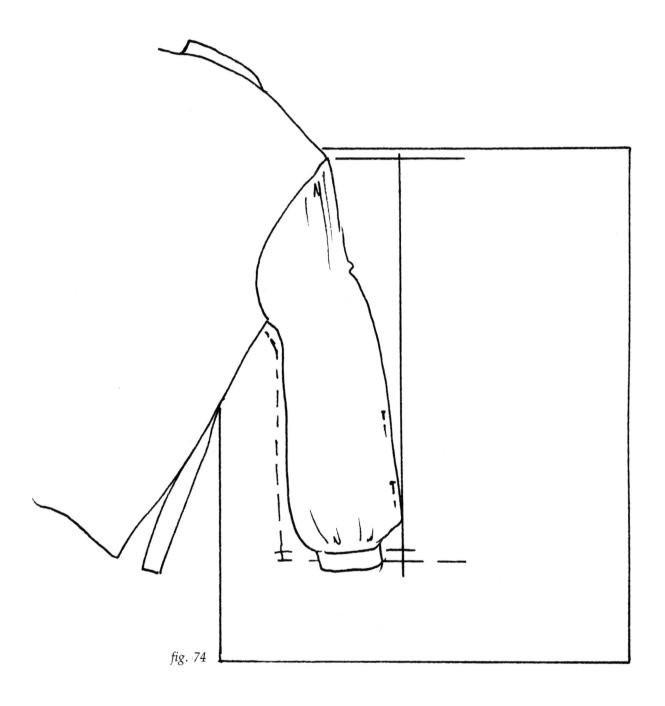

fig. 74

Now fold the garment back to expose the shape of the armhole curve (fig. 75). This curve is the shape of the cap or top of the sleeve. Draw the line from the point that you have marked at the center top and continue around the curve. This is the adjustment for ease at the sleeve top. The drawing will appear larger than the actual sleeve, but don't let it deceive you. You will be checking this sleeve against a commercial pattern piece, when you complete the outline.

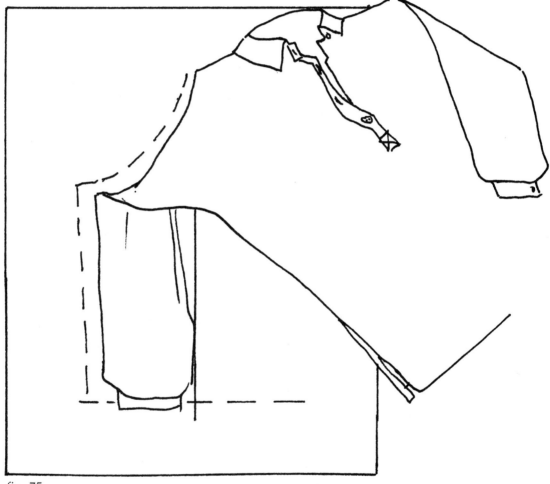

fig. 75

Continue sketching the line around to the point where the underarm seam of the sleeve meets the side seam of the shirt. You have now drawn half the sleeve pattern. Draw the *center line*; it will be used to align the other half of the sleeve.

STEP 2

Reverse the shirt, placing the pinned fold of the sleeve on the *center line* you have just drawn (fig. 76). Keep the bottom edge of the sleeve in a straight

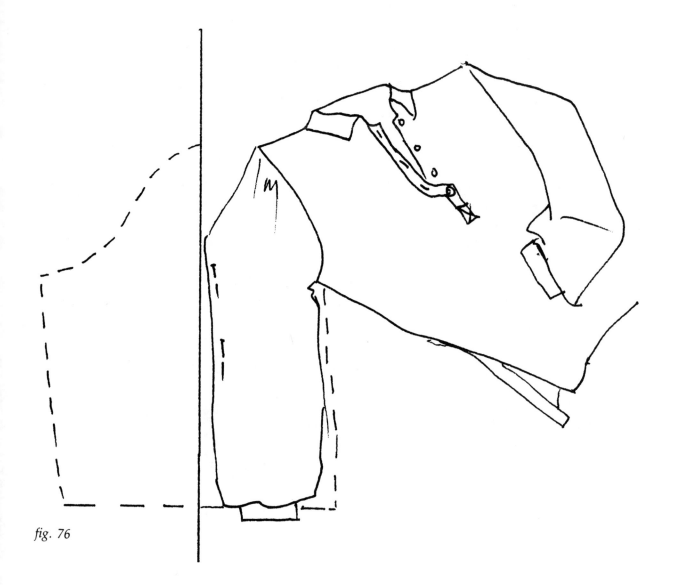

fig. 76

line with the bottom edge of the section already drawn. Complete the lines of the bottom edge plus hem allowance of the lower part of the sleeve; continue marking the line up the seam edge to the end of the seam. Now fold the garment over the sleeve to expose the other half of the armhole curve and complete the drawing of the other half of the sleeve cap (fig. 77). Remove the garment and check the sleeve cap to be sure that it is properly rounded.

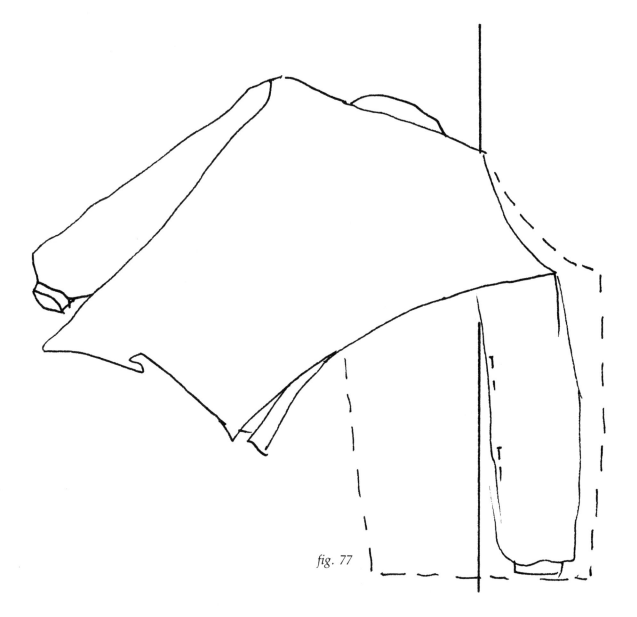

fig. 77

STEP 3

Compare the length of the pattern piece you have just drawn with the length of the actual sleeve. This will tell you if you had the sleeve completely straight and flat when you drew the outline, and if you have included enough ease. You can also compare the finished sleeve pattern to a commercial pattern piece. This type of comparison is reassuring and helps build confidence in your ability to draft patterns. Any necessary adjustments can then be made before the pattern is finalized (fig. 78).

CODING THE PATTERNS

Label this piece with the same information that was used for the body of the shirt: *date, size, shirt, sleeve* and *cut two*. Be sure you specify which edge of the sleeve is the *front* and which is the *back*. The back of the sleeve has additional ease for movement; if the sleeve is not put in correctly, the front will be too large and the back seam could pull out at the first wearing.

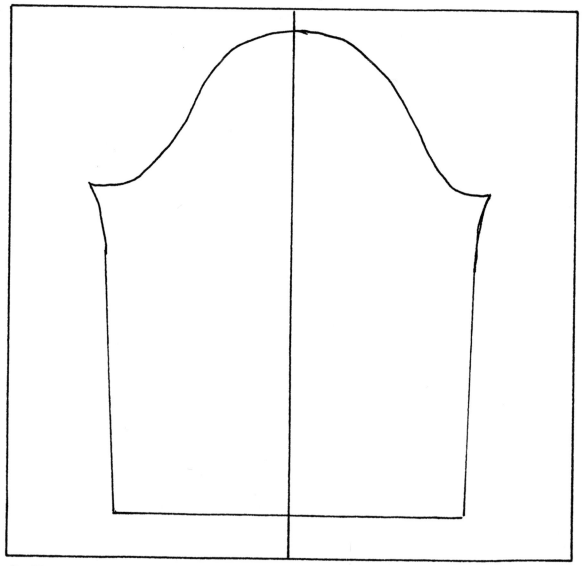

fig. 78

Collar

The survey of this garment determined that the collar was slightly shaped instead of a straight piece, like the cowl neckline of the garment in the preceding chapter. A curved collar is used on garments that call for a close, smooth fit around the neckline. This collar will need a separate pattern piece. It cannot be made from a measurement notation. Your pattern paper should be generous enough to extend well beyond the height of the collar to allow for the slope of the lower edge that attaches to the bodice. As with the other pattern pieces, the paper should be twice the width of the collar with the *center line* clearly marked.

STEP 1

Fold the collar in half, matching the front points (fig. 79). Place the fold of the collar on the *center line* and sketch around the outer edges (fig. 80). Mark the lower or seam edge and fold the collar down to expose this line (fig. 81). Sketch the curve of the lower edge. Remove the garment from the pattern. To complete the outline of the entire collar, use one of the following methods: (1) fold the pattern piece along the *center line* and trace the other half of the collar from the first part that you have just drawn; or (2) turn the garment over and draft the other part of the pattern directly from the garment. Either way works, but tracing the original part is probably easier.

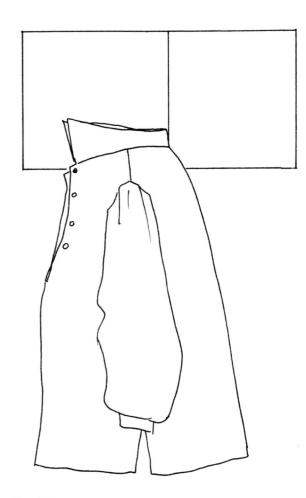

fig. 79

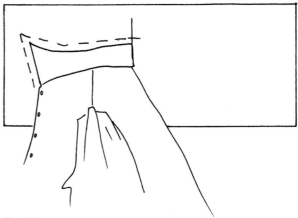

fig. 80

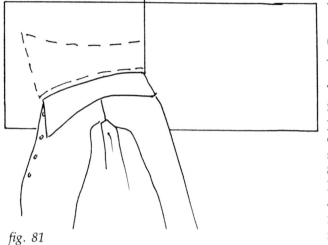

fig. 81

STEP 2

Compare the pattern piece you have just drawn with the actual collar to be sure you have drawn it high enough to fold properly. Complete roughing the lower seam allowance and finalize the lines. Mark the lower edge where the collar meets the shoulder seam and identify the *center back* (fig. 82). Code the collar pattern with important details.

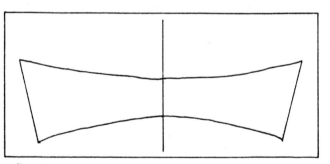
fig. 82

GENERAL INFORMATION

Detail your sewing instructions on the *front* or the *back* of the pattern (see page 54). Be sure to indicate *cut two* on the collar (the second collar is the facing) and the sleeve patterns. Measure and note the front placket with the other details (it is a straight piece and does not require a separate pattern). Be sure the seam allowance was added to all pattern pieces.

Using Your Pattern Creatively

This pattern would make a wonderful **windbreaker** if cut from nylon (fig. 83). For additional warmth, you might line it in flannel. Make it reversible by cutting the garment from two different fabrics and sewing these together along the outer edges (fig. 84). To make it reversible: Cut the pattern one size larger by adding ¼ inch (6 mm) all the way round to allow for the additional bulk. Sew each side separately. Place the two sections with right sides of the fabric together; stitch all the way round the outside edges, leaving an opening of 3 to 4 inches (7.6 to 10.2 cm) at the bottom. Turn the windbreaker through this opening to the right side; use a few hand or machine stitches to close the gap. A drawstring can be added to the bottom to keep in your body heat. If using it for active sportswear, give the windbreaker a spray of waterproofing. Grip fasteners could be substituted for the buttons on the original garment. They add a very sporty touch and are available in many colors and designs.

Make it in wool or melton cloth, for a wonderful cold-weather **pullover jacket** that can be belted over skirts or pants for a more fitted look (fig. 85). Lengthen the pattern to coat length, 1½ to 2 inches (3.8 to 5.1 cm) longer than your usual skirt length. The garment can be slit along the center front from the neck opening to the hem. A placket can be added down the entire front and the coat can be lined for very cold weather wear (fig. 86). Facings can be created by tracing off the shape of the fronts, allowing about 4 inches (10.2 cm) for the width.

This pattern also works well as an **unlined coat**. Bind off all seam edges with matching or contrasting strips of fabric. Be sure to finish off your seams to avoid fraying. Seams will be visible without a lining to hide them. Eliminate the collar for a cardigan look: Wrap a matching scarf around your neck for wintertime chic and warmth. Add patch pockets and belt the sleeves, for a more tailored finish.

For a lovely **reversible coat** for cold weather: Cut the pattern twice from contrasting wool, creating two separate coats. Put the two garments with right sides of the fabric together. Carefully match the

fig. 83

fig. 84

fig. 85   fig. 86

shoulder seams, neck points and all outer lines. Stitch around the entire outside edges, leaving a small opening at the bottom through which you can turn the completed garment right side out. After turning it right side out, press the seamline. Close the opening with a few hand stitches. Topstitch around the entire outside of the coat for a firmer finish. This technique, lining to the edge of the outer shell, is called edge-lining.

You can make **long** or **short dresses** from this pattern. Make a floor-length dress from wool jersey. Wear it belted or unbelted for at-home entertaining (fig. 87). As a street-length dress, bound in leather, you have an elegant garment for luncheon or office (fig. 88). With roll-up sleeves and an obi sash (that you could embroider or decorate with jewels), this garment could be the most versatile one you own (fig. 89). Make a matching jabot to button down the front, or ruffle the neckline as we did for the first basic pattern.

fig. 87

fig. 88

As you draft your pattern you may get some ideas to modify the original design. Make a note of these ideas on a corner of the pattern (these fleeting thoughts can be very elusive). Take another look at Using Your Pattern Creatively (page 34) at the end of the preceding chapter. Any of those ideas could apply to this pattern.

fig. 89

Direct-Cut Method and Additional Thoughts

The system for drafting a pattern from a garment with set-in sleeves has now been described for you as simply as I could. By using it, this technique can become an integrated part of your sewing skills. You will hardly remember a time when you couldn't draft a pattern from a finished garment.

I must now admit that I don't always draft a pattern to cut a garment or create a design. Often, I feel that the design I am working on will be a "one-shot proposition," and the general dimensions will give me everything I need. I simply lay out the fabric on my cutting board or on the floor and plan the placement of the various pieces from the finished garment, as I would the placement of pattern pieces. I then direct-cut the new garment from the existing one.

Sometimes, I even use sections of several garments to achieve the look I want. The concept outlined in this book is all I need, whether I draft a pattern or direct-cut. Knowing how I want to assemble the pieces, I can create a garment on my cutting table, take the pieces to my sewing machine and wear that new garment the same evening.

To do the same, you must know your body and your figure problems very well. Draft your patterns honestly. If your hips measure 38 inches (96.5 cm), don't cut pants or straight skirts that will only fit round a fence post. Skinny little garments look great on the cutting table, but whom will they fit? A tight garment will only make you look larger. The garment that fits you properly will flatter you, whatever your size.

One's taste is usually established in the late teens. Enjoy the garments that please you and don't let the current fads force you into clothing that is not for you. Those style trends that were in your closet in the past and are still showing up, with some variation, should lead you in the direction of your fashion future. Accumulate patterns that you will be making exclusively for yourself and file them carefully. These are some of the components that are interchangeable for your future wardrobe. The rest will come from the clothing itself.

As I've been telling you, a pattern doesn't have to be used exactly as it was drafted. That four-gore skirt of wool flannel that you enjoy so much could easily become an eight-gored skirt of chiffon, if that is how you would like to interpret it. The cotton shirtwaist dress that you took a pattern from last summer could easily become a silk crepe dinner dress this winter. You're only limited by your imagination, what you see in the stores and all the help you can get from fashion magazines.

All of this maneuvering of pattern pieces and ideas might even stir your memory. There may have been a commercial pattern that you bought some time ago that you suddenly remember for its beautiful sleeve or unusual pocket treatment. Use those pieces with the patterns that you are currently drafting. Just because you didn't draft it doesn't mean that you have to throw it away!

For more detailed information about figures, proportion and fabrics, refer to Fashions, Fabrics & Figure Types (page 9).

Remember, a garment that fits well can become a pattern that does not have to be altered. A pattern that fits well is the height of personal style.

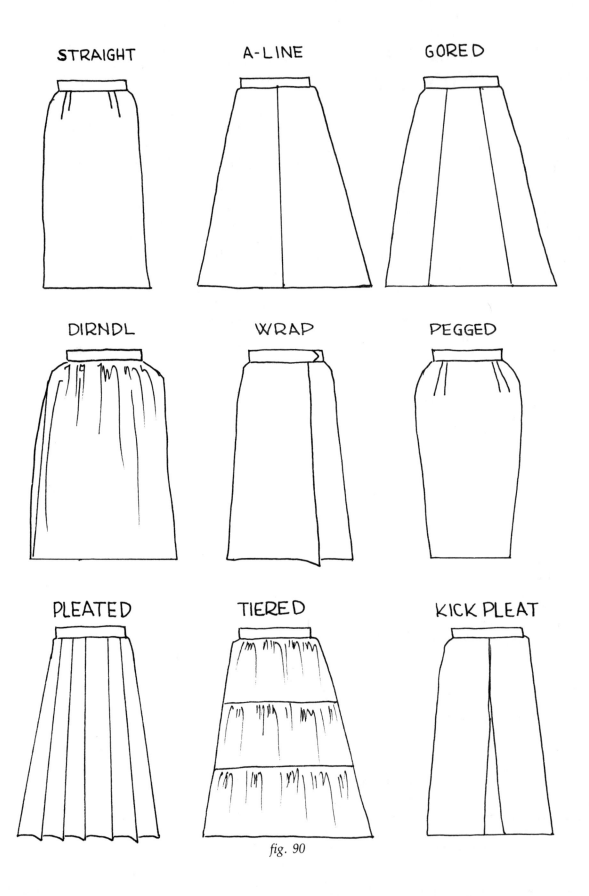

STRAIGHT

A-LINE

GORED

DIRNDL

WRAP

PEGGED

PLEATED

TIERED

KICK PLEAT

fig. 90

SKIRTS

There comes a time when we are finally pried loose from the comfort of our well-worn jeans, a time when we must don a skirt or dress and show legs above our shoe tops. Let's prepare for that traumatic moment by adding a few of these unfamiliar items to our wardrobes.

Skirts come in such a variety of styles; there are enough to please each of us. There are straight, peg-topped, A-line, gored, wrap, dirndl and gathered skirts. The list is almost endless. And, as for the length, your skirt can be above the knee or down to your shinbone and still be very stylish. We have finally reached a time in fashion where hemlines can be any length you find comfortable (fig. 90).

Skirts are not only the mainstay of a wardrobe, they are the transitional garments for seasonal dressing. Take a skirt out of the closet and you can coordinate your own "look" while still dressing comfortably.

A wool tweed skirt combined with a cotton shirt or a sweater is versatile enough for you to wear and meander through a shopping mall, a country lane, go to the office, an early dinner date or an important meeting (fig. 91). Combine that same skirt with a silk shirt or blouse and you're ready for cocktails. Team it with a sequined top, and you're dressed for an evening date, a trip to the theatre or even a dinner dance.

fig. 91

Choose a denim skirt for a walk on the beach or the foundation of your wardrobe for a weekend trip. It will combine with anything from leotards, flats and sweat shirts to sheer hosiery, dress shoes and silk shirts (fig. 92).

A skirt can take the place of many dresses in a business wardrobe. It can combine with contrasting blouses and sweaters for seasonal comfort. By matching your skirt and top in both fabric and color you can create the look of a dress while maintaining the convenience and versatility of separates (fig. 93).

fig. 92

If you plan to be married soon, consider a white or ecru silk skirt and matching top. These pieces can be worn after the wedding is over instead of being tucked away in a box, waiting to become a family heirloom (fig. 94).

Skirts are probably the easiest garments to sew.

fig. 93

fig. 94

The process is as simple as gathering a straight piece of fabric, adding pockets and an elastic waistband, machine-sewing a hem and donning the completed garment in about an hour (fig. 95). You can also lay out your fabric and cut a new skirt from an existing one without first cutting a pattern.

You probably have at least one skirt that you've been saving for years that may never fit you again. Somehow, you can't seem to part with it. If you really love the style, make a pattern from it. You can then alter the length and size, creating a sloper that will fit your figure and current life-style.

Let's take a look at such an item (fig. 96). This comfortable, straight skirt dates back to the days of the Beatles and minis. Its length is terribly dated and the width appears at least two sizes too narrow, but the basic design is attractive and flattering. This is the type of skirt that I want in my wardrobe today and tomorrow. I kept promising myself that some-day I'd draft a pattern from it. Since I am familiar with my preferred skirt length and I know my hip and waist measurements, I'll be wearing the style in next to no time.

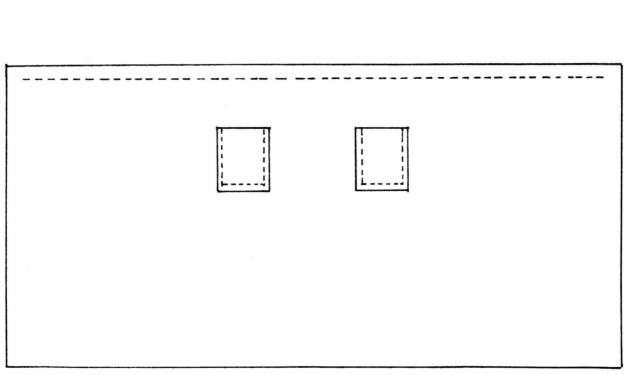

fig. 95

fig. 96

SURVEY: SKIRTS

Critique this garment as you did the previous ones. This is a very important step that should be repeated each time you select a new garment for pattern drafting. The more familiar you are with the garment, the easier it is to achieve a good, working pattern.

Survey Questions: Skirts

1. Does this skirt still fit you or will you have to make changes in width, length or both?

2. What is the style of the skirt (dirndl, wrap, straight, gored, other)?

3. How many pieces will this pattern call for?

4. Is this skirt cut on the lengthwise grain or on the bias?

5. How is the waistband attached?

6. Where is the closure? What type of closure?

7. How many darts? Placement?

8. Are there pleats or attached facings to plan for?

9. Will this pattern need additional ease for other types of fabric?

10. Does the skirt have pockets? How many? Where? How are they applied?

The survey revealed that the top of this skirt has two darts, a fly front and a center seam. Until now, we have discussed two-piece patterns: front and back. This skirt pattern will obviously call for a change as the garment has a two-piece front. Since both halves of the front are the same, we will only have to draw half the front section.

There are no pockets in this skirt. Never knowing what to do with my hands or handkerchief without pockets in my garments, I will indicate a placement for them on the pattern. To do this, I will either take some measurements from another skirt or copy the location from the tunic top (page 32) by matching the waistlines and drawing the marks at the point where the pockets appear on that garment. Since arm lengths vary considerably, make sure your pocket location is at a comfortable level for *your* use.

Try on the skirt that you will be using for your pattern. Check it for width and length (fig. 97). If the skirt has been stored for a long time, it probably won't fit properly. If it is just a matter of length, you can adjust the length as you rough-in the hemline. If you've changed more than one size in width since you last wore this skirt, be prepared for additional adjustments. A good rule of thumb is to add approximately ¼ inch (6 mm) to the width at each side of a pattern piece for each additional size of the finished garment (fig. 98). For each additional ½ inch (13 mm) of width on each side (2 sizes), add ¼ inch (6 mm) at the top of the skirt to keep the darts

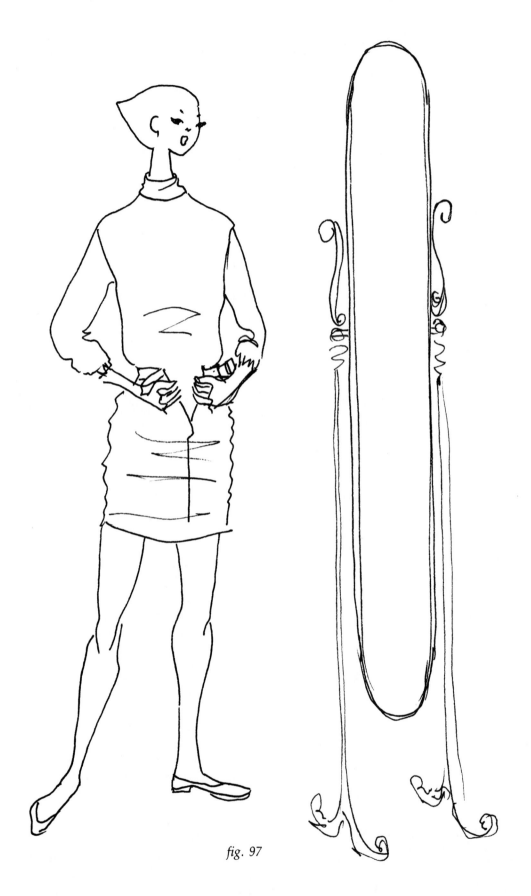

fig. 97

and hipline curve in proper adjustment with the rest of the garment. If the original skirt is a size 12* and you are now wearing a 14, just add ¼ inch (6 mm) to each side seam to achieve the additional room you need. If the original skirt is a 12 and you need a 16, add ½ inch (13 mm) at each side (2 sizes)

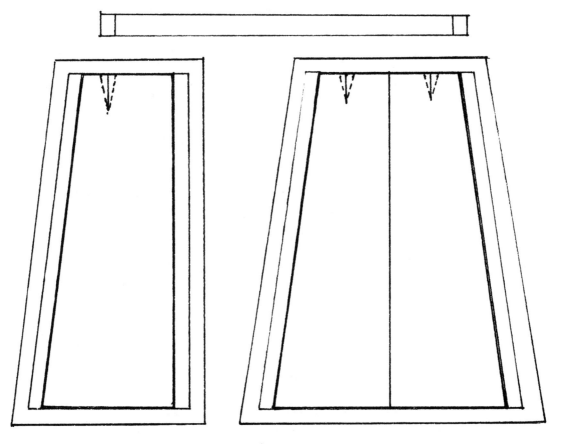

fig. 98

*Women's Clothing Conversion (dresses and suits)

U.S.	10	12	14	16
U.K.	32	34	36	38

and ¼ inch (6 mm) at the top of the skirt to readjust the darts (fig. 99).

If you're one of the lucky ones who has lost weight and kept it off, you will be taking off ¼ inch (6 mm) at each side of the pattern piece for every size you've lost.

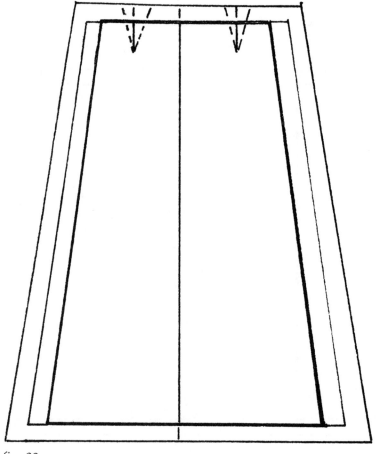

fig. 99

Step 1—Back

Lay the skirt, back side up, on the pattern paper. Allow enough pattern paper at the hemline to include your chosen street length plus any additional hemline measurements that you might want, such as maxi and floor length (fig. 100). For a better view of the construction details, turn the skirt inside out. Straighten the outer seam lines and waistband.

Make any necessary size corrections before you start your rough draft. Start the pattern by sketching the outer seam edge of each side from the hem to the widest part of the hip (fig. 101). Don't draw the line to the top of the garment until later, when you indicate the allowance for the darts.

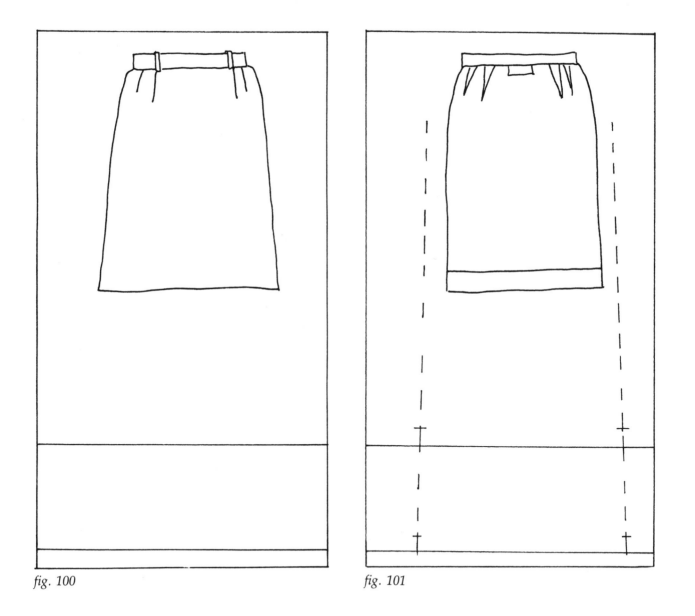

fig. 100   fig. 101

DARTS

Fold the waistband inside the skirt to expose the top of the skirt and placement of the darts. Mark the middle or fold line of the darts (nearer the middle of the skirt) with a slash (fig. 102). Mark the sewing lines by drawing an additional slash at each side of the fold line. Allow the same amount of space between the darts as on the original skirt. Repeat for the outside darts starting from the sewing line. The width of each dart is the amount to be added to the outer edges of the skirt at the waistline (fig. 103). Taper the outside seam line to meet the line you have already drawn to the widest point of the hip.

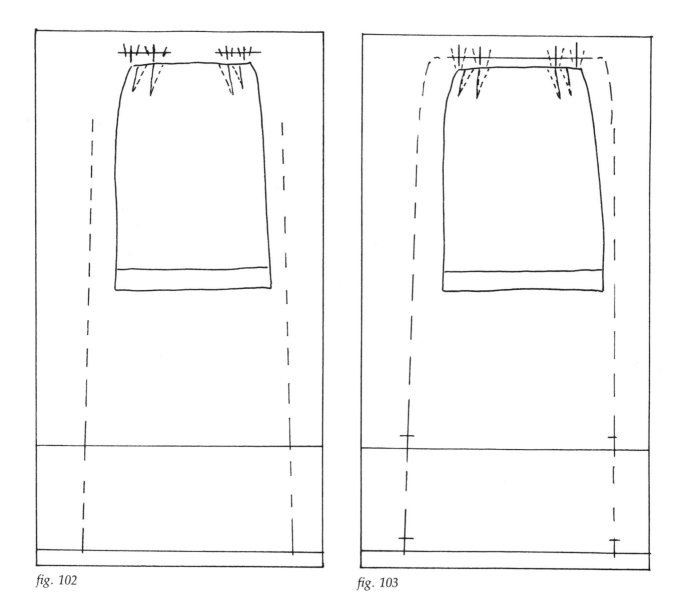

fig. 102

fig. 103

Sketch the hem allowance at the bottom of the skirt. Before you remove the skirt from the rough pattern draft, mark the bottom of the dart on the pattern by folding the skirt lengthwise along the fold of the dart, exposing the lowest point (fig. 104). Complete drawing the darts between the points indicated.

Fold the pattern in half lengthwise, matching the side seams to find the middle of the pattern piece and draw this line. Compare the two halves to be sure your markings are the same for both sides. Finalize all pattern lines (fig. 105). Code the pattern and lay it aside.

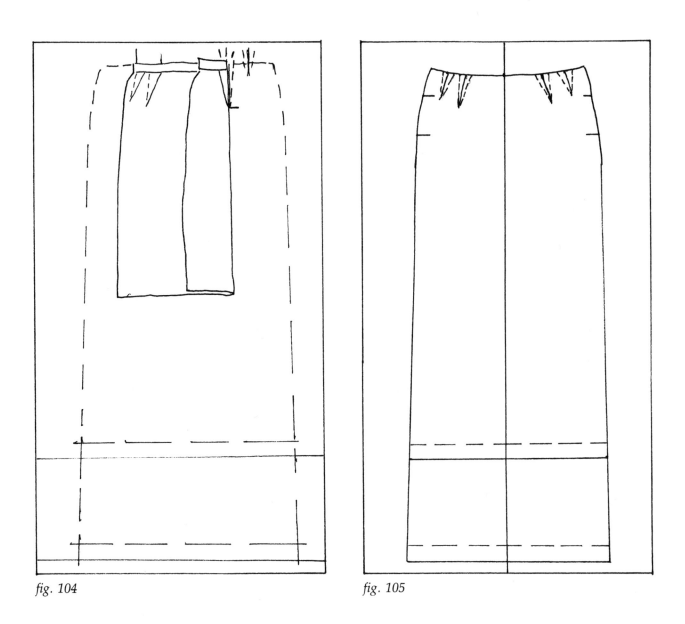

fig. 104   fig. 105

73

Step 2—Front

Fold the skirt along the center-front seam. Lay it on a fresh piece of pattern paper with the waistline near the top. Leave enough room to add the seam allowance (fig. 106). Be sure the pattern paper is long enough to include the various lengths that you added to the *back*. When you use it, the pattern can be folded up for cutting the shorter lengths.

Starting at the center front, sketch the seam line from the top where it crosses the waistline to the bottom or hemline. To indicate the extension for the fly, mark the width of the facing from the point where it crosses the waistline to the lower edge where it cuts back across the center-front seam (fig. 107).

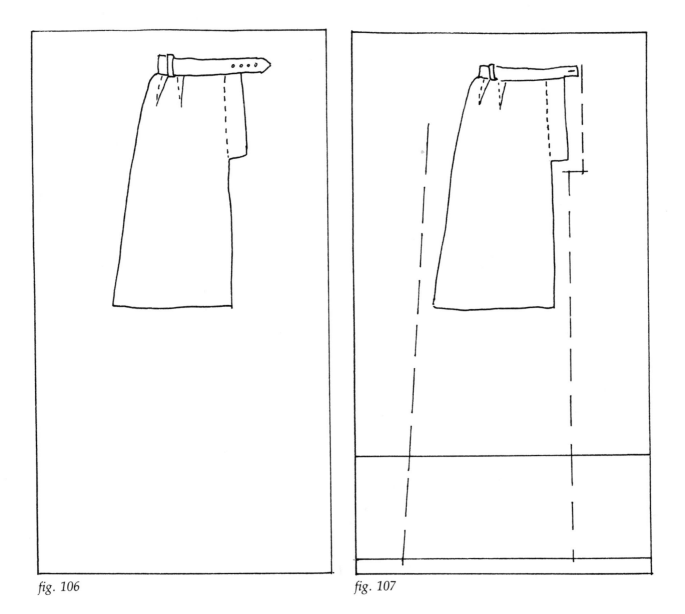

fig. 106   fig. 107

Sketch across the waistline to the fold of the first dart. Mark this point and indicate the stitching lines as you did for the back. Slide the skirt to the place where the stitched dart meets the outer drawn point (fig. 108). Now draw the next section and repeat the procedure for the next dart. When complete, finish the sketch of the waistline to the outer edge. Add the width of the darts to the outside seam edge. Taper the line to the point of the widest part of the hip (fig. 109). You have now added the necessary room at the top of your skirt to allow for the darts. Mark the outer edge of the waistline and continue down the outside seam to the hem. Add the hem allowance and continue across the bottom edge. Mark the pocket placement.

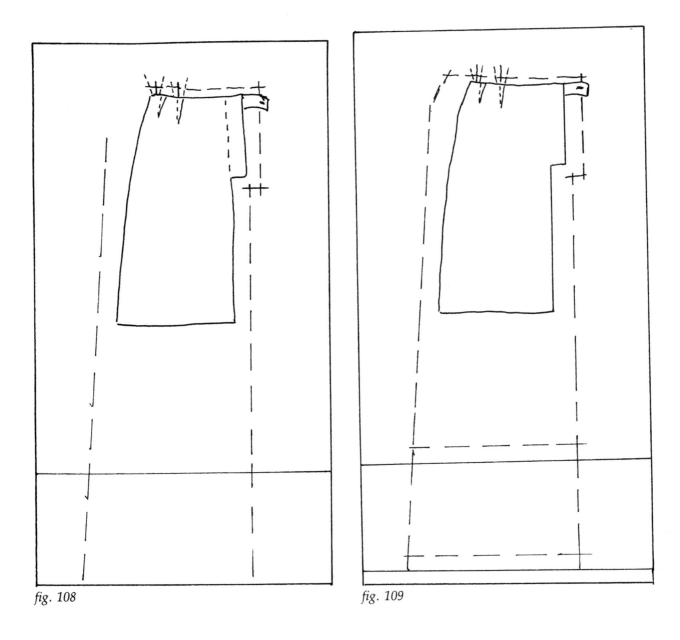

fig. 108

fig. 109

Remove the skirt from the pattern piece and finalize all lines with contrasting pen. Make sure you have included your seam allowance with the drawing of the pattern pieces. Write all information and code the pattern. Indicate whether this pattern was drafted from a woven or knitted fabric garment.

There is no need to draw the opposite half of the pattern front. Both halves of the front can be cut from this one pattern piece. Just reverse the pattern for the left and right halves. The fly extensions should be cut for both sides of the front; the underneath extension will act as a backing for the zipper (fig. 110).

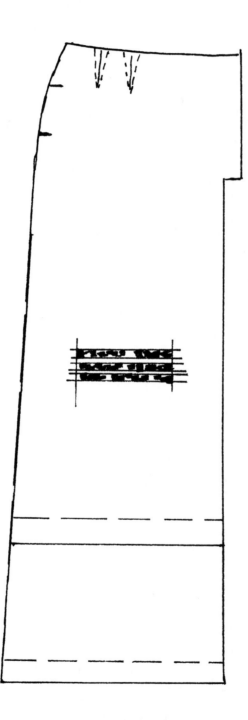

fig. 110

When you draft a pattern for a garment with an asymmetric front or back, a pattern should be made for each section (fig. 111).

The center seam of a straight garment must be parallel to the lengthwise grain for the garment to hang correctly. Cutting off-center will cause any garment to pull. A straight skirt will ripple at the hem and bag severely at the seat and tummy, clinging to your leg on one side and flaring out at the other. A blouse or dress can pull the buttons and bunch to the side. To keep your garments in perfect alignment: (1) check the grain lines of the garment you're using before drafting the pattern; (2) note the grain lines on the patterns; (3) before you cut, check the positioning of the pattern on the fabric.

SEWING THE SKIRT

Stitch the darts from the widest point to the narrowest to ensure the dart's smoothness. Don't back-tack at the bottom of a dart as this could pull up the point causing a buckle at the bottom. Tie the thread ends into a square knot and trim the excess thread. When you have finished all darts on the open or unsewn sections of the skirt, attach the pocket sections to the unseamed pieces. There is less weight to juggle and less bulk to cope with before assembling the skirt (see Inseam Pockets, page 32).

Look through your commercial patterns and you will find sewing directional arrows. Notice that most garments are sewn from bottom to top. This means of sewing seems to keep the seam flatter and smoother. Sewing with the grain of the fabric also seems to result in the least amount of fraying at the seam edges.

Wrap Skirts

Wrap skirts are a delightful addition to any wardrobe. They can hang as slim as a reed and still provide plenty of room for comfortable walking. They are easy to make from almost any kind of pattern: straight skirt, A-line, gathered or dirndl. Wrap skirts are also very easy to cut directly from a finished skirt, eliminating a pattern completely (fig. 112).

When you decide that a wrap skirt is the style for you, decide what type of "look" you're after. These

fig. 111

skirts are wonderful for any hour of the day or night—easy to put on in the morning for breakfast, comfortable for entertaining or going to the market. Certainly, wrap skirts are appropriate for the office and can take you dinner-dancing in the evening when made in appropriate fabrics. In other words, wrap skirts are the ultimate answer for practicality and comfort.

For active sports, choose a skirt that is either slightly A-line or dirndl style to provide maximum comfort for your activity. Since sports activities don't leave your hands free for carrying a purse, plan a pocket style and size for your needs. Include these details in your new garment. To make them shadowproof, wrap skirts should be backed (fabric

fig. 112

and lining sewn together), lined (skirt and lining constructed separately and then stitched together) or made reversible. You won't have to worry about slips or petticoats under your skirt and when the wind blows, you'll show the contrasting lining under the skirt.

For office or general wear, back or line your wrap skirt. It will hang better and wrinkle less when you sit.

Long wrap skirts for evening wear should not be backed if they are made from soft fabrics because you will lose the soft, flowing look of the finished garment. Either line them with a soft fabric or wear a separate slip.

Any skirt style can be reinterpreted into a wrap skirt. Decide whether you want the garment to wrap in the front or back. The larger piece should be cut first. Our sample skirt wraps in the back (fig. 113).

fig. 113

Lay the fabric out on the work surface and fold lengthwise with the selvages together. Be sure the fabric is wide enough to accommodate the width of the folded back or front of the skirt. Now fold the skirt in half lengthwise, matching the side seams and enclosing the back of the garment inside the front (fig. 114). Lay the skirt with its center fold on the fold of the fabric. You will have enough fabric left to cut the waistband and the tie ends of the skirt (fig. 115) by using the selvages for the inside portion of the band. As you cut, allow for the darts and seam allowances.

When you have cut this section of the skirt, unfold it and turn it over to cut the back. Open the fabric out flat, not folded in half. The fabric width will not accommodate both back sections in a side-by-side placement or on the fold. Each overlapping back section will be approximately three-quarters of

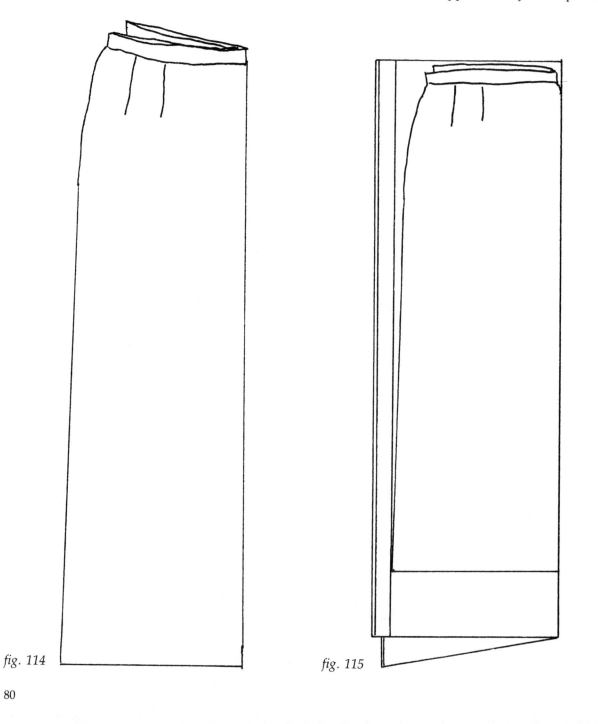

fig. 114

fig. 115

the entire back section of the original skirt plus the facing. Facings are cut as extensions with each back panel.

Lay the back of the skirt right side up on the lengthwise grain of the fabric with the section from the dart to the side seam folded under (see fig. 104). Cut the panel on the lengthwise grain of the fabric using one selvage for the straight edge of the facing (fig. 116). When you have completed this section,

turn it over on the remainder of the fabric and cut the other half of the back. Remember, this must be reversed to provide a left and right overlap for the back of the skirt (fig. 117).

Choose the pocket style that you prefer. Cut and stitch pockets to the skirt (see Inseam Pockets, page 32, or Patch Pockets, page 112). Complete the darts, then the side seams.

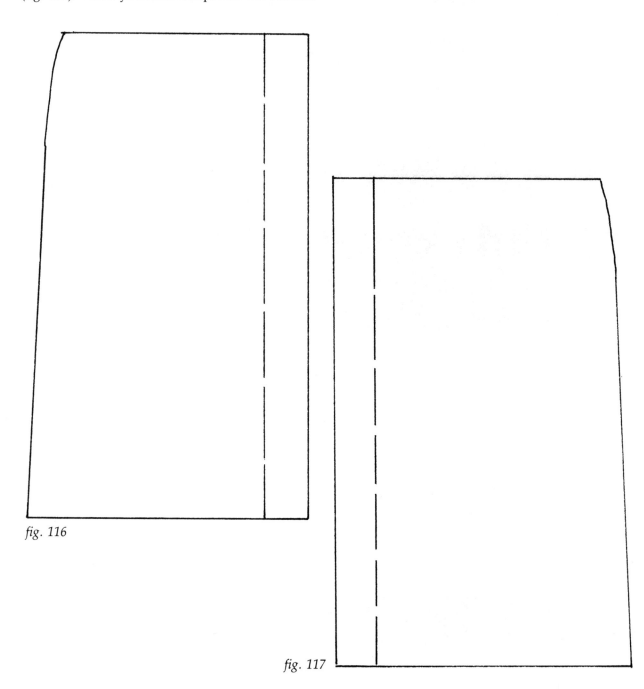

fig. 116

fig. 117

For the waistband, cut a piece of the same fabric. It should be 2½ to 3 inches (6.4 to 7.6 cm) wide and long enough to go completely around your waist with enough left over to tie or close in the manner you prefer. Plan about 24 to 30 inches (61 to 76.2 cm) beyond your waistline measurement for tying a nice bow (fig. 118). If your remnant is not long enough to cut the entire length of the waistband, try cutting it in three sections. Match the waistband seams to the side seams of the skirt. A waistband with two piecings puts the seam at the center front—not a very attractive result.

fig. 118

Interface the waistband section that fits around your body, but don't interface the tie ends. Interfacing makes a bulky bow. Stitch the ties into a tube and turn them right side out. You can either leave them plain or topstitch them (fig. 119).

The waistband can also be secured with hooks or buttons. Cut the waistband 2 or 3 inches (5.1 to 7.6 cm) longer than your waistline measurement. Sew the band to the skirt in the conventional manner and complete it with button and buttonhole (fig. 120).

If your fabric is opaque—denim, double-faced cotton, twill, etc.—you can just topstitch around the outer edges of the skirt, attach the waistband and you are finished. There's no need to line or back heavy fabrics. They will stand up well by themselves.

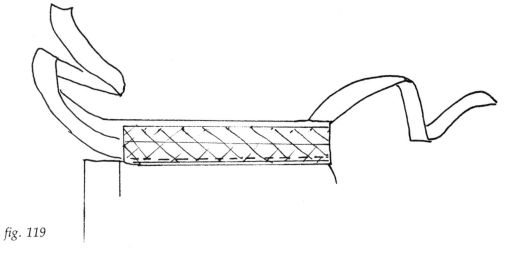

fig. 119

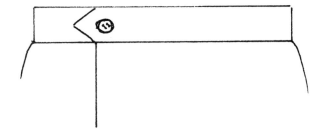

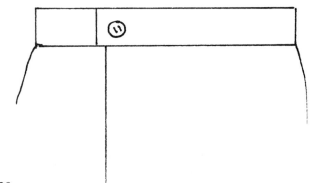

fig. 120

REVERSIBLE WRAP SKIRTS

Lightweight fabrics can appear flimsy or transparent when used alone. Combining two layers of thin or sheer fabrics will produce an attractive wrap skirt with enough body to hang properly. And it will have a totally different look on each side. Cut the pattern twice—the first from the chosen surface fabric and the reversible side from a contrasting fabric. Stitch the pockets to each skirt. Then stitch the side seams. The result is separate pockets for each side of the reversible skirt. If you feel that this might be too bulky in your selected fabric, plan for patch pockets that will be stitched directly to each side of the skirt fronts. Stitch the darts and side seams separately for each skirt. Place the two skirts with right sides together. Stitch completely around the outside of the skirt—down one side, across the bottom and up the opposite side. Turn right side out, then attach the waistband (fig. 121). Your wrap skirt is ready to put on.

fig. 121

FRONT WRAP SKIRTS

Wrap skirts work just as well wrapped to the front rather than to the back (fig. 122). Reverse the procedure you just completed and cut the *back* on the fold. The front then becomes the two-piece section and is cut in the same manner described above for the back. For an attractive touch on a front wrap, round the corners rather than cutting the hem straight across the bottom. To create the facing for

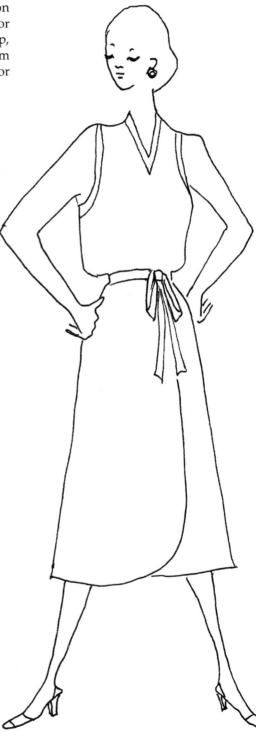

fig. 122

this skirt style, lay the front on the fabric and cut a facing approximately 3 to 4 inches (7.6 to 10.2 cm) wide for the ends and bottom of the front. If you allow the facing to meet the side seams, the curve at the hem will never curl. You will need a facing for each side of the skirt front (fig. 123).

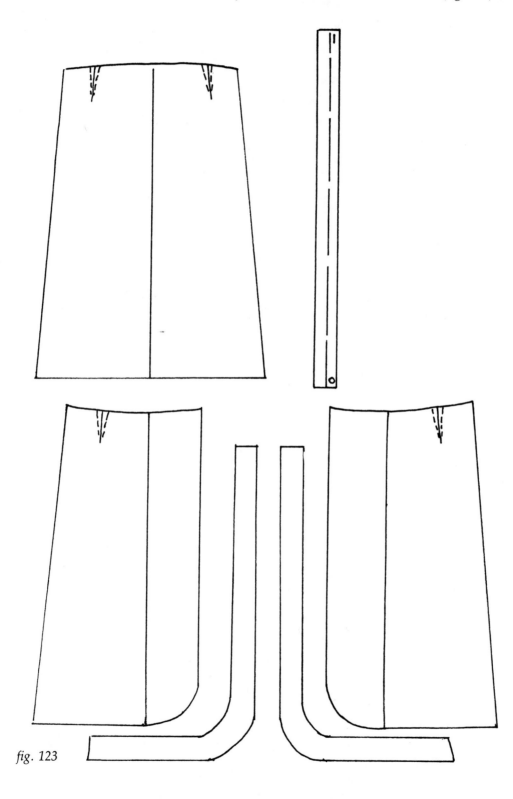

fig. 123

A-Line Skirts

Any straight skirt can be changed into an A-line by merely swinging the pattern out approximately 4 inches (10.2 cm) from the center line (fig. 124).

Place the pattern (or skirt, if using the direct-cut method) on the pattern paper and draw the waistline. Mark the darts, if there are any. Sketch the line from the waist to the widest part of the hip. Then, move the pattern out 2 to 4 inches (5.1 to 10.2 cm) from the center (depending on how much width you need). Complete the outside seam line to the hem. Smooth out any dip that might appear where the two sections meet. Repeat for the other side. Front and back patterns are done by the same method. Mark the closure, indicate the pocket openings, other details and code the pattern. The pattern's ready to use.

fig. 124

Dirndl Skirts

Dirndls are probably the easiest skirts in the entire book of sewing (fig. 125). To make one, place any straight skirt on your pattern paper. Mark the top and add 2 to 3 inches (5.1 to 7.6 cm) to each side of the waistline. Mark your preferred hem length. Add 3 to 5 inches (7.6 to 12.7 cm) to the width of the hem (fig. 126). Curve the waistline up from the center to meet the new side-seam markings for the front. Repeat the process for the back. Check all pattern lines and details, adding hem and seam allowances. The drindl style looks elegant when cut a little longer than your usual length. It will hang nicely and be comfortable for sitting and walking.

fig. 125

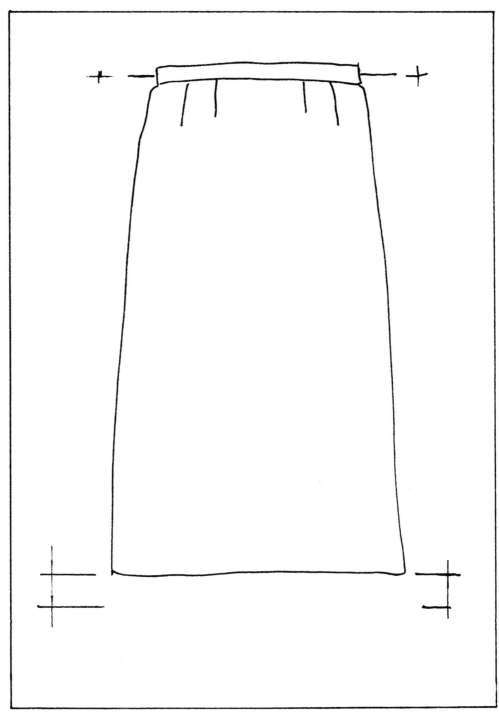

fig. 126

Tulip Skirts

You can create this pattern from a straight-skirt pattern (fig. 127). This style is not particularly flattering if you don't have a good figure and well-shaped legs. This hemline really draws the eye to the hips and legs!

Choose a pattern with a one-piece front and a one-piece back. Trace the pattern onto a fresh piece of pattern paper. You really don't want to cut up a working pattern. Measure approximately 2 inches (5.1 cm) above your kneecap (fig. 128), and draw a line across the pattern at that point. Repeat the marking on the pattern front and back.

Start working with the front section of your pattern. Divide the waistline at the darts and cut straight down through the fold of the dart to the hem (fig. 129). This creates three panels from the

fig. 127

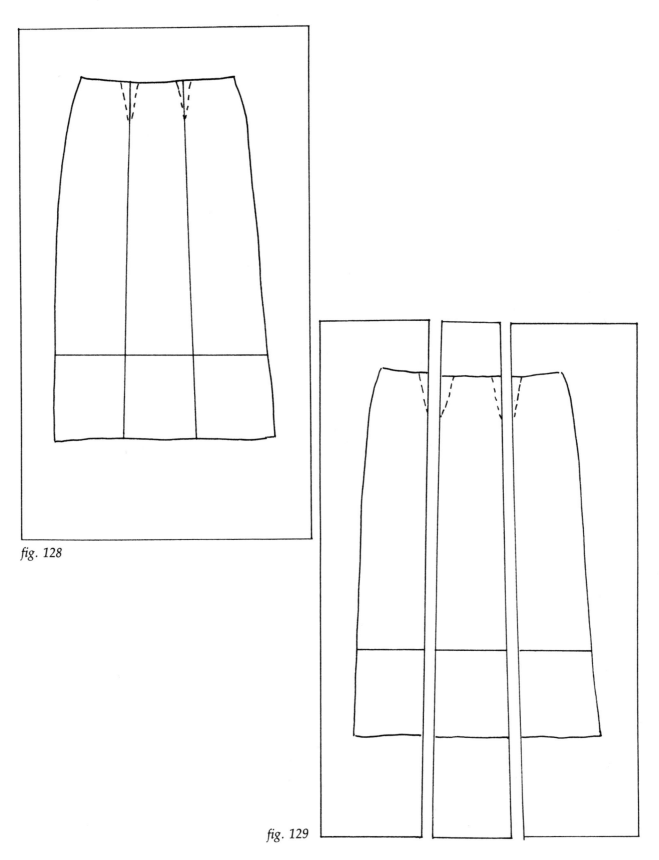

fig. 128

fig. 129

front section. Immediately label them: *left front, center front* and *right front*. (You don't want to get these sections mixed up.) Tape an extension to each pattern piece along the sides (fig. 130). It should be long enough to cover the length between the line you drew above the kneecap and about 7 inches (17.8 cm) wide. Extend the hemline out about 4 inches (10.2 cm). (This figure is a variable depending upon your height and weight and how flouncy you want your skirt.) Angle the line up to meet the

line above the kneecap (fig. 131). This line can either be drawn straight or curved slightly to meet the existing line. Add a seam allowance to the upper section or, as a reminder, indicate on the pattern that the seam allowance was not included. Any pattern that does not include a seam allowance can be cut ¼ inch (6 mm) outside the pattern to allow for stitching. Repeat the process for each panel at both sides. Complete the back.

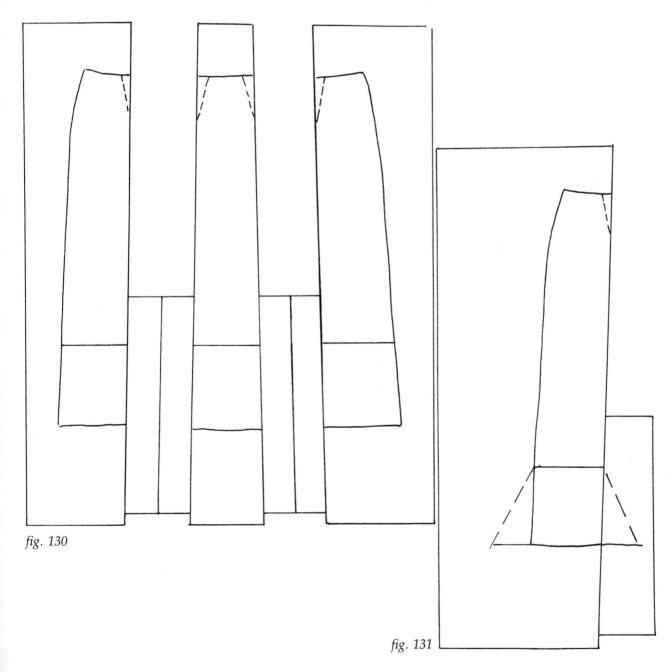

fig. 130

fig. 131

92

There is an additional treatment for this skirt that is truly delightful. Curve the hem of each panel to create a "tulip petal" look for your skirt (fig. 132). An irregular hemline is very dressy and fun to wear. Create a template of heavy paper or cardboard and use it to draw the outline of the curve consistently or make a compass with a piece of string, a hatpin and a piece of chalk or soap. Secure the string to the pin and stick it into the hemline at the middle of the panel (fig. 133). Measure the string for the distance between the hatpin and the outside seam line of the panel. Secure a bit of soap or chalk to the string end. Pull the loose end round in a half circle, marking the curve. You can also tie a knot at the loose end of the string, using it as a marker for the length. Insert a pin through the fabric at several points to define a cutting line. When the entire section is marked off, cut along the marked line. You can also use a large plate as a guide to sketch the line. To finish the hemline, sew a narrow, rolled hem.

fig. 132

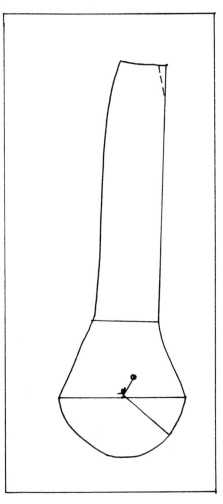

fig. 133

Another interesting treatment with this pattern is to design a handkerchief hemline (fig. 134). Find the center point of the panel along the hemline and measure down to the length you'd like for each point, such as floor length or ankle length. Draw a line from each seam edge to meet at the low point in the center (fig. 135.) A handkerchief hemline is effective on either daytime or evening dresses. It is fresh and new when done in soft wool, with satin ribbon binding the hemline. This technique also works well when sewing with chiffon or silk.

Try the tulip style not only with taffetas and other dressy fabrics, but also with sweat-shirt fabric—a feminine change from warm-ups and sweat suits (fig. 136).

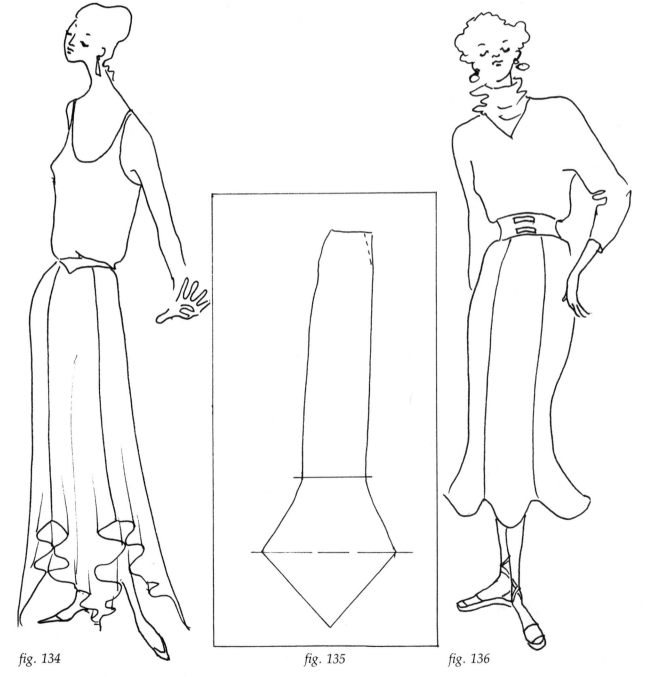

fig. 134   fig. 135   fig. 136

Gored Skirts

Gored skirts are begun very much like the tulip skirt, but the horizontal mark is drawn at the widest point of the hip. Each panel will flare slightly from that point to the hemline.

Make another copy of your straight-skirt pattern. Cut through the fold of the dart to the hemline to create three panels from the skirt front (fig. 137). Label each section: *front left*, *front center*, *front right*.

To create the A-line shape of each panel, lay the right front panel on a piece of pattern paper of equal length. Mark an extension for the hemline out 2 inches (5.1 cm) beyond the existing line. Draw a connecting line between this point and the widest part of the hip. Repeat at the opposite side of the panel. Add the hem facing and draw the angle of the seam line for the bottom (fig. 138). Repeat the instructions for each panel. When you stitch the skirt, be sure to retain the angles you drew for the hemline to make the hem fall into place without ripples.

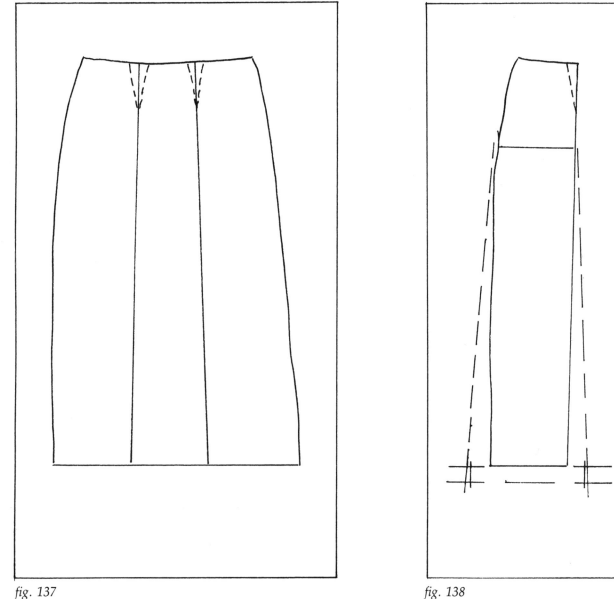

fig. 137   *fig. 138*

Pleats

You can create an inverted pleat at the center of a straight skirt by drawing an extension at the *center-front* line (fig. 139). If your fabric is wide enough to cut the front in one piece, carefully mark the fold lines for the pleat with chalk or soap. Fold the pleats and press firmly before you stitch the skirt (fig. 140). Secure the pleat folds at the waistband. Either leave the entire pleat open or topstitch down to a comfortable point for you (fig. 141).

If the fabric isn't wide enough to hold the entire pleat extension, cut a two-piece front. Add a seam allowance to each side of the fold line. Attach the underfold as a separate piece (fig. 142). When adding more than one pleat (fig. 143), mark your fabric with three parallel lines for each pleat (fig. 144). These lines should be approximately 1½ inches (3.8 cm) apart. Each pleat will add 4½ inches (11.4 cm) to the width of the pattern section. A pleated skirt may be hemmed before the waistband is attached. Straight-hanging hemlines and pleats are assured by making final adjustments from the top of the garment.

Sew one side seam. Complete all but a small section of the hem at each side (fig. 145). Fold and firmly press the pleats. The pleats may be edge-stitched for a crisper finish. Insert the zipper and stitch the other seam. Complete the open section of the hem. Pin the skirt to the waistline and try it on. Make any adjustments to the hem or hang of the pleats. Attach the waistband and button and complete the buttonhole.

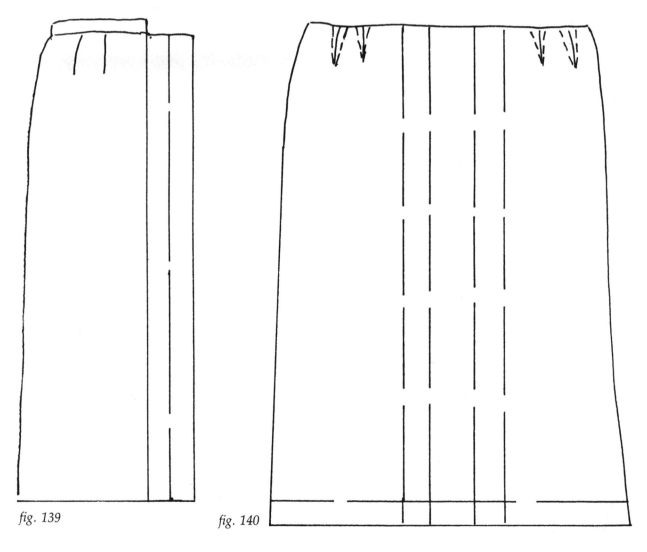

fig. 139

fig. 140

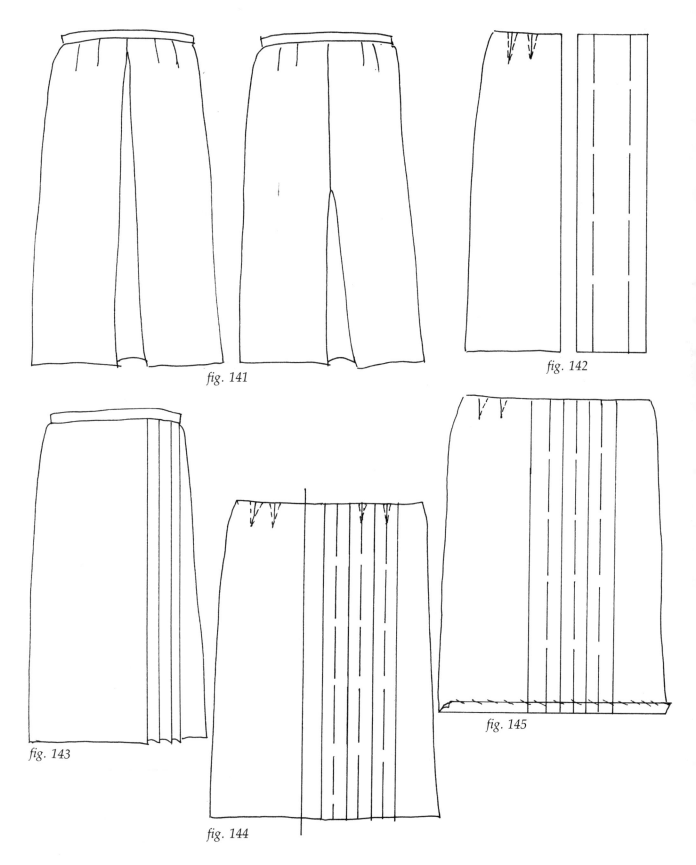

fig. 141

fig. 142

fig. 143

fig. 144

fig. 145

GODETS

Instead of a short pleat at the lower end of the skirt you might make a godet—a bias wedge, semicircle or rectangle that is inserted into the seam or slit (fig. 146). The godet provides extra room at the hem and adds a little dash to the garment.

ALTERATIONS

By now, I'm sure you are aware of your skirt length for various styles. When you lay out a skirt to draft a pattern, always check the length of the garment you are using before you draw the hem on the pattern. A fashionable length for your hemline is anywhere that *you* find it comfortable.

fig. 146

Most of our fitting problems stem from the difference between waist and hip measurements. The "average" figure is supposed to have a 10-inch (25.4-cm) difference between these measurements, but how many of us actually do? Too often we must alter a purchased skirt before a first wearing, usually because when we fit the hipline, the waistline is much too big. To adjust the fit, remove the front of the waistband and make the darts a little deeper. Instead of a 1½-inch (3.8-cm) dart, make each one 2 inches (5.1 cm) or more, depending upon the amount of difference between hips and waistline. If the difference between the two measurements is too great, create an additional dart at each side to pick up the excess, shorten the waistband and ease it back onto the garment. When altering your own patterns, follow this same system.

If your tummy is rather round, take most of your additional room at the front of the garment rather than the back (fig. 147). With this problem, you usually don't need as much seat room. By increasing the darts slightly, your waistband will fit properly and there won't be any wrinkles below the waist or the tummy.

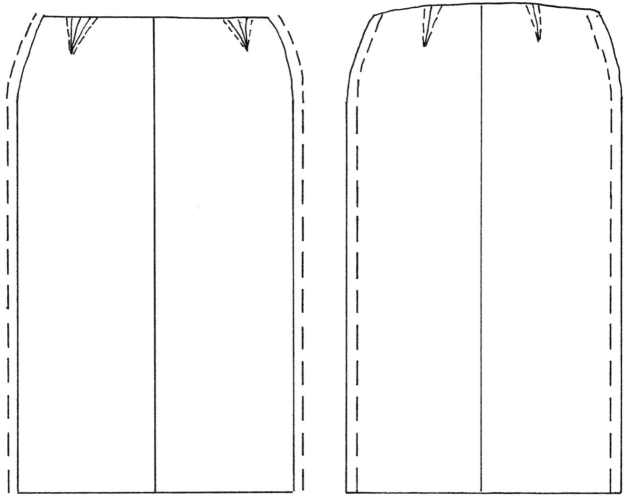

fig. 147

With heavy thighs, a slightly pegged skirt will give you room for a smoother line. Build some roundness into the silhouette by angling the outside lines of the garment up from approximately mid-thigh past the widest point of the hips. Continue the line straight up to the waistline (fig. 148). This is a very handsome style that can be very slenderizing. The hemline can be quite narrow and still give you plenty of room in the hip and thigh area.

For swayback problems, gently curve the center-back seam while stitching (fig. 149). As you sew across the waistline, bring the seam line down into the body of the garment about ⅛ to ¼ inch (3 to 6 mm) at the middle of the waistline. This will remove any potential bulge from the small of the back. If you are making the correction on the pattern, lower the center back of the waistline by ⅛ to ¼ inch (3 to 6 mm) and gently curve the line up to meet the top point of the side seams at each side. The easiest way to fit a skirt or trousers when dealing with swayback problems is to cut a piece of grosgrain ribbon the length of the waistband and pin it around the waistline. Pin the skirt or pants (with all darts and seams completed) to the outside of the ribbon. Make adjustments while viewing yourself in a three-way mirror. This ribbon then becomes the facing for the waistband. Just cut a single waistband (including a seam allowance on each side) and stitch it over the grosgrain ribbon. No need to interface the band.

fig. 148

fig. 149

Using Your Pattern Creatively

Almost any style of skirt can be successfully varied in length and fabric. These changes will obviously create the new mood of that pattern. Any of the wrap skirts could be lengthened to the floor, cut from crepe (silk or wool) and become an elegant dinner skirt.

Adding facings to the side of a straight skirt and securing it with buttons or snaps would certainly create a whole new look for the original straight-skirt pattern (fig. 150). Gabardine would be seasonally versatile. This style could enhance any jacket or blazer.

Decorative finishes for skirts can be as creative as you desire. Embroider or appliqué any type of pattern or design on the garment (fig. 151 and 152). You are only limited by your imagination. If the skirt is to be worn on the golf course, you might want your hem to read, "Hole out all putts" or "Keep all carts off the greens." For tennis, you might want to say "The court is reserved for two hours" or "Last month I had an A-rating." What is your favorite quote? Gag line? Slogan?

Put one or two large patch pockets on your wrap. Decide how big you want these to be and just cut out the squares. Cut each one double to give it strength and sew the pocket together. Top-stitch to apply.

If you decide to appliqué on the skirt, cut all pieces for the design and machine-stitch them to the panel or panels before the skirt is stitched together. This means much less bulk for you to handle. If the pattern is to slide across more than one panel, sew the necessary sections together before doing the decorations.

Try to store several skirt lengths in your fabric cache to put together something for emergency use. Remnant shopping can keep this stash current with the seasons.

Just a few additional notes on skirts. Knitted garments are usually the fastest to make. They don't require zippers or other closures. A simple elastic waistband and a machine-sewn hem can finish them off nicely. These usually become favorite "make in one hour" skirts.

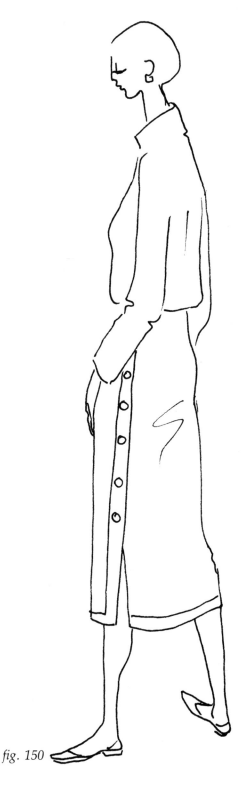

fig. 150

Dirndls and drawstring skirts are probably the next on the "most popular" list because they don't require any amount of fitting and are loose and comfortable for summer wear. Scraps from other garments can be sewn together to make attractive patchwork dirndls. Patchwork clothing is fashionable. "Crafted" items seem to draw admiration.

fig. 151

fig. 152

PANTS

The fit of a pair of pants is probably the most talked about subject among people who sew. The most common problems are pants that would fit the waist but won't pull up over the hips and thighs, or, if they can be pulled up and buttoned, they can't be zipped. And we shouldn't forget the pants that fit the hips beautifully but have approximately 12 inches (30.5 cm) of extra fabric at the waistline. There are also the pants that seem to be even too short to be considered good hip-huggers. Then, there's the most deceptive pair of all: pants that seem to fit everywhere, except the crotch hanging halfway to your knees. Have we mentioned your prime problem? From these complaints we must conclude that there are two major categories for this subject: (1) pants that were purchased that don't fit; (2) pants that were made at home that, also, don't fit.

On rare occasions we find a pair of pants with that elusive quality—*fit*. In our enthusiasm over this minor miracle, we wear the precious garment until it is threadbare. This puts us back to square one, making the rounds of sewing, shopping and agonizing, trying to find pants that fit.

The logical solution to this madness is to take that properly fitting pair of pants to the cutting table and draft a pattern. In this manner, the fit of those treasured pants is yours, as often as you feel like making a new pair. The results you get from your sloper or personal pattern will always be consistent with the original pants.

As a home sewer you know that woven and knitted fabrics have totally different properties. Woven fabric is made up of warp (lengthwise) and filling or weft (crosswise) threads woven on the loom. When woven closely, the fabric is firm. The ease and shape of pants made from woven fabric must begin with the *pattern*. The design must have darts or pleats to fit the hips and waistline, ease built into the crotch, inseam lines to allow room for sitting and walking and a placket or closure for access to the pants. In other words, the pants must be curved to conform to the shape of the body. If they are too loose, pants of woven fabrics will sag and droop; if too tight, pants develop "smile" lines at the seams, or the seams pull and break.

Not so with knitted fabrics. Knits are forgiving and flexible. Most knits are created from stretchy yarns that are looped around needles, allowing additional flexibility to the yarn beyond the generic properties of the fibre. Knits conform to your body and require little shaping for a good fit. For this reason, most knitted pants are pull-ons, because the fabric will stretch to go over the hips.

Choose a suitable fabric for your pattern. For instance, when commercial patterns read "*for knits only*," the patterns have no ease and very little shaping, and are not suitable for woven fabrics. Knitted fabrics used with these patterns will follow the curves of the body and take on the shape of the wearer. I recommend two basic pants patterns: one for knits and a second for woven fabrics. These slopers will have one line in common: the crotch-rise seam. This is the line where the fit begins.

Pants range from very short athletic shorts to wonderful, sweeping palazzo pants—"grand entrance pants"—that flow around the ankles, nearly touching the floor as you walk into a room. These styles, and variations, can be interpreted from the two basic patterns you draft in this chapter. We will vary the length and width of the legs, create new body styles and learn a few tricks for attaching waistbands and installing zippers that you might not have known before—all this without having to make any additional patterns or pattern pieces. You will be able to make a selection of fashionable pants, each with a perfect fit. Let's delve into the entire spectrum of pants from waistline to hemline . . . wherever that might be.

Choosing a Garment

Just as the first pattern we drafted was taken from a simple T-shirt, the first pants pattern will be drafted from a simple pair of knit pull-on pants without any detailing—no darts, pleats or ease and little, if any, shaping (fig. 153). You will, no doubt, recognize some of the following information as drafting a pattern from a pair of pants is similar to taking a pattern from a garment with sleeves.

SURVEY: KNIT PANTS

Let's get acquainted with the pants we've chosen. The survey questions below will lead us to the information we need to draft this pattern.

fig. 153

Survey Questions: Knit Pants

1. Waistband: What type of waistband is on the garment, elastic or firm?
Elastic: How wide is the elastic? How is it attached?
Firm: How is it interfaced? How is it attached? What type of closure is used?

2. Pockets: How many pockets? What style? Placement?

3. Shaping: Is the top darted or pleated?

4. Legs: Are the legs narrow or full? How are they shaped? Is the bottom cuffed or cut straight? Does the crease follow the lengthwise grain of the fabric? Is the crease pressed or stitched?

5. Front/back: Note the difference between back and front. How much higher is the center/back than the side seam edge? How much lower is the center front than the side seam edge? How much difference is there between the width of the front and back?

A survey revealed the following information:

- Style: Simple pull-on trousers with straight legs and no shaping.

- Waistband: Attached with elastic encased. No closures of any kind.

- Pockets: Two, inseam.

- Legs: Straight, no cuffs.

PREPARATION

Your worktable should be adequate to accommo-date the pants without any part of the garment hanging over an edge. Pants pattern lines are critical and any part of the garment hanging over the edges of the table could distort the entire pattern by pulling that section of the garment out of line. If your table cannot hold the entire garment, move to the floor.

The pattern paper should be long enough to cover the length and wide enough to cover the crotch line or widest part of your pants pattern. Work from either the left or right side of the garment, whichever you find most comfortable (fig. 154).

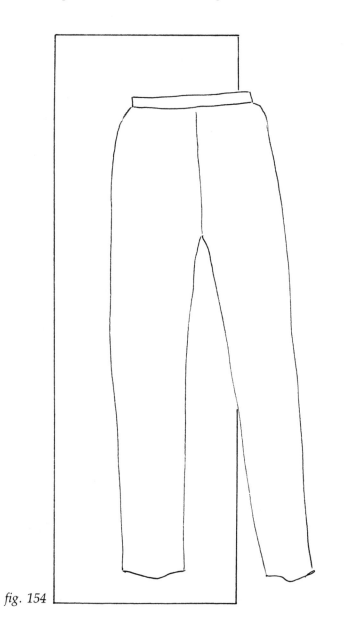

fig. 154

Front: Knits

Place the garment *front* side up on the pattern paper. Straighten all seams; be sure that the legs are smooth and flat on the surface. Sketch the outside seam line straight up from the bottom of the leg to the widest part of the hip and continue up from this point to the top without indenting at the waist (fig. 155). When sewing this garment, the excess fabric will be eased into the waistband. The extra room is necessary to pull the pants on over the hips without stretching them completely out of shape or breaking the stitching at the top.

Fold the waistband inside the garment and mark the waistline and seam allowance. Continue across and indicate the point where the front rise (center front) crosses the waistline. Mark the crease line for the center of the leg at both the top and bottom of the pattern (fig. 156). The crease line is the *center front* or lengthwise grain for laying out the finished pattern for cutting. Always observe this line carefully, or your garment could hang lopsided.

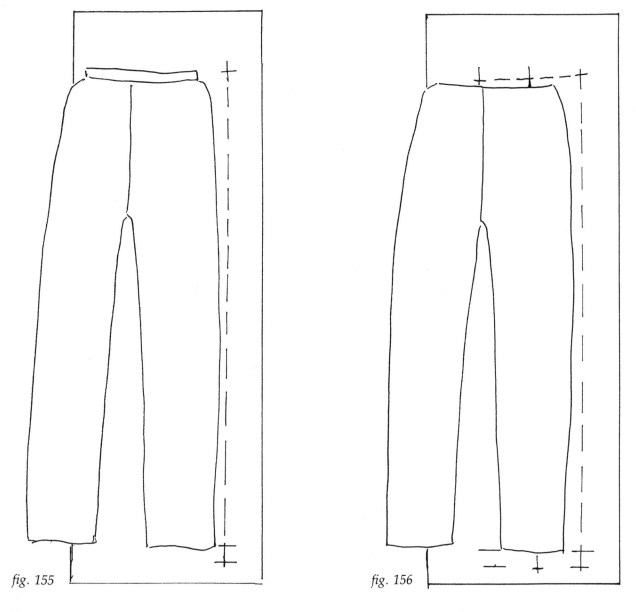

fig. 155

fig. 156

Sketch the fold line and hem allowance at the bottom of the leg and continue the rough outline up the inseam to the bed (seat base) of the crotch. Mark this point (fig. 157).

Remove the garment from the pattern and turn the opposite leg inside out. Pull the first leg through and into the reversed leg as you would to sew the crotch seam. Straighten the crotch-rise seam carefully and place the pants, back down, on the pattern paper, aligning the seam with the marks you had previously drawn for the waist-rise and crotch-inseam points (fig. 158). Rough-in this line between the indicated marks.

Finalize all lines and identify the markings. Name and date the pattern piece and detail all information for future use, including *knits only*. Be sure to note the size of the pants used for drafting the pattern and your current weight. This is more critical with pants patterns than any other garment. If your weight should vary by five pounds in either direction, you might need to make some pattern adjustments. It is certainly more logical to know that before you cut into your fabric.

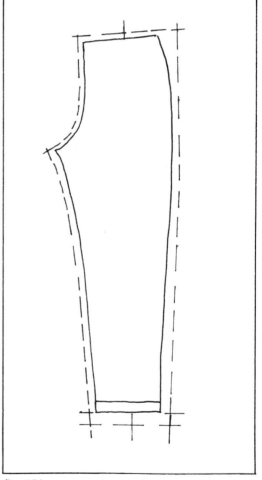

fig. 158

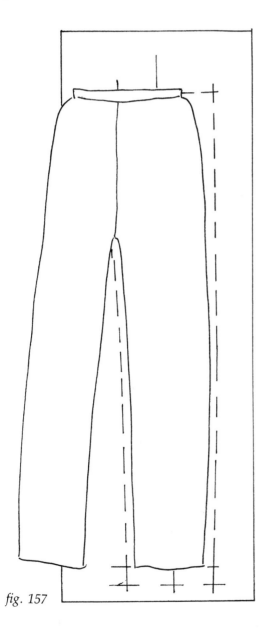

fig. 157

Back: Knits

When you did the survey for your pants you should have discovered a difference in width between the back and the front. The back of a pair of pants is always a little wider than the front to allow for body movement and ease. As the garment is already inside out, take a good look at the construction details. Place the garment, front side up, on the table or floor to get a clear view of the difference between the front and back (fig. 159). Since the back is a little wider, the excess fabric will roll to the top or front of the garment. Measure the actual amount of

extra fabric for the back and be sure to include half of it at each side of the leg when drafting the pattern. Check the upper part of the back between the waist and crotch. If additional fabric appears in this area, be sure to add an equal amount to your pattern. Do not divide this amount between the front and back but add all of it to the back where it belongs. This shaping is vital to the fit and hang of the pants.

Lay the garment on the pattern paper, back side up, marking the waistline, hem fold and facing. Draw straight up from the widest part of the hip to the point where the side seam crosses the waistline (fig. 160). Suggest the waistline and indicate the point where the center back and waist meet. Mark

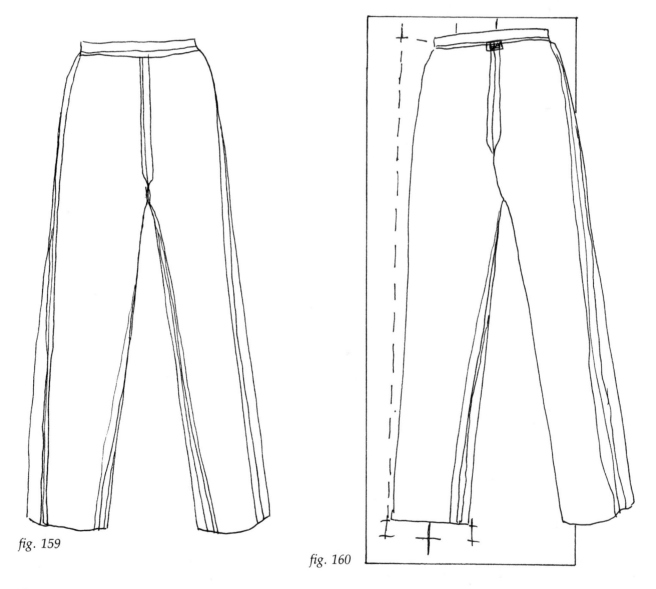

fig. 159

fig. 160

the inseam and locate the spot for the beginning of the crotch. If the pants are not already inside out, reverse them, pulling the opposite leg into the one you've been working on. Place this curve of the crotch-rise on the pattern between the marks for the waistline and inseam lines (fig. 161). Sketch this line. It should angle out slightly from the waist, slope below the crotch shelf and rise slightly to meet the point of the inseam.

Check your drawing carefully. The outside seams of the front and back should be of equal length. The waistline should curve gently downwards at the center front to accommodate the curve of the waistline and slightly upwards at the center back to allow for sitting ease, without pulling the back of the waistband down to the buttocks when seated (fig. 162). The center back might rise as much as 1 inch to 1¾ inches (2.5 to 4.4 cm) above the side seam points while the center front could be ¼ to ¾ inch (6 to 19 mm) lower.

Finalize all lines and complete pattern notations and sewing directions. Note the length of elastic needed for the waistband. This is about 2 inches (5.1 cm) less than your actual waistline measurement for a comfortable fit. (If your waistline has a tendency to change, remeasure the next time you're using the pattern. Elastic should fit firmly and comfortably.)

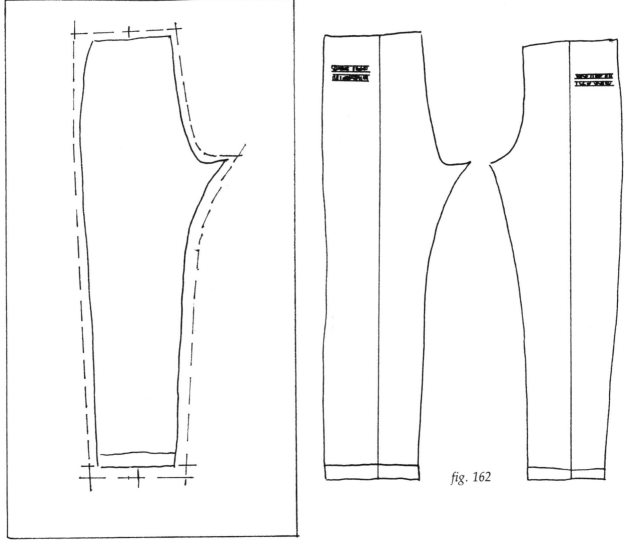

fig. 161

fig. 162

CONSTRUCTION

The first time you use this pattern, cut it just as it was drafted but leave some room at the top, above the waistline, for final adjustments of the crotch seam.

Stitch the crotch-rise seam first, both front and back, and then sew the inseams of each leg. Put a

elastic ends together over the garment to hold it in place. Pull the crotch up, snug to your body by grasping the center seam at the waistline and adjusting it until it is seated properly. Do not pull the side seams higher than the center front to ensure the fit of the legs and a smooth hang of the pants (fig. 164). If you see diagonal creases rising from the crotch, the side seams are too high. If the creases are

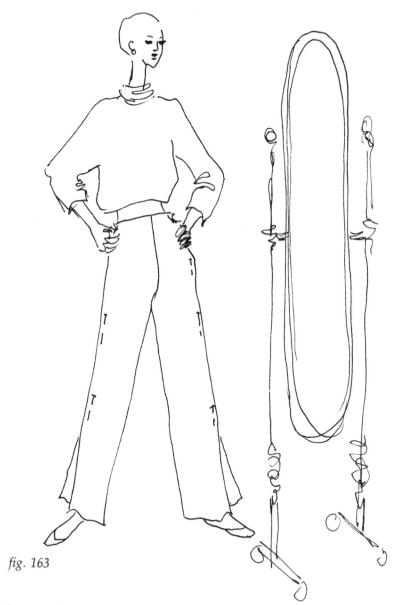

fig. 163

few pins along the outside seam line to hold the garment together (fig. 163). Cut a piece of elastic 2 inches (5.1 cm) less than your waistline measurement and find a large safety pin. Put the pants on. Wrap the elastic strip around the waist. Pin the

pointing down the legs, or if the legs appear to be on the baggy side, the side seams should be pulled up a little. (This is why I suggested leaving a little extra fabric at the top of the pants when cutting the sections.)

To indicate where your waistline is located, either mark the garment with a sliver of soap (which will rub off the fabric as you sew) or put pins in the fabric at the lower edge of the elastic. If there is enough fabric left at the top, it can be turned over the elastic and stitched, eliminating the need for a separate waistband. Adjustments made on the garment should be transferred to the sloper for future use.

more body to the garment. This also makes the garment a little smaller to compensate for the looseness of the knit. A less stretchy fabric requires only a ¼-inch (6-mm) seam stitched with an overlock or serge stitch, which closes the seam and overcasts the edges at the same time. For a decorative finish, seams can be made on the outside of the garment, using serge or zigzag stitching.

fig. 164

When making pants from this pattern, note the width of the seams and the type of fabric used when adjustments were made. A soft, thin fabric, such as cotton single knit, might hang better with a ½-inch (13-mm) seam that can be topstitched, giving a little

To add inseam pockets, see page 32. This simple method can be used for any garment. When sewing inseam pockets into garments with waistbands, catch the upper edge of the pocket into the waistband as it is attached.

Patch Pockets

Patch pockets work well for casual pants. The size will vary, depending upon the size of your hands and the type of pants you're making. Gardening pants call for deep pockets that can hold your tools. Tennis pants need pockets deep enough to hold the balls with ease.

When using lightweight fabric, cut two rectangles of an appropriate size for each pocket (fig. 165). Lightweight fabrics need support, so one rectangle will serve as the lining. Or, use lining fabric for the underside. With right sides together stitch rectangles from the center top to the center bottom, leaving an opening at the center bottom to turn the pocket to the right side (fig. 166). Trim the corners. Turn the pocket to the right side and topstitch the upper edge, before attaching the pocket to the garment. Topstitch the pocket to the pants about ¼ inch (6 mm) from the edge along three sides, reinforcing the top corners at both edges (fig. 167).

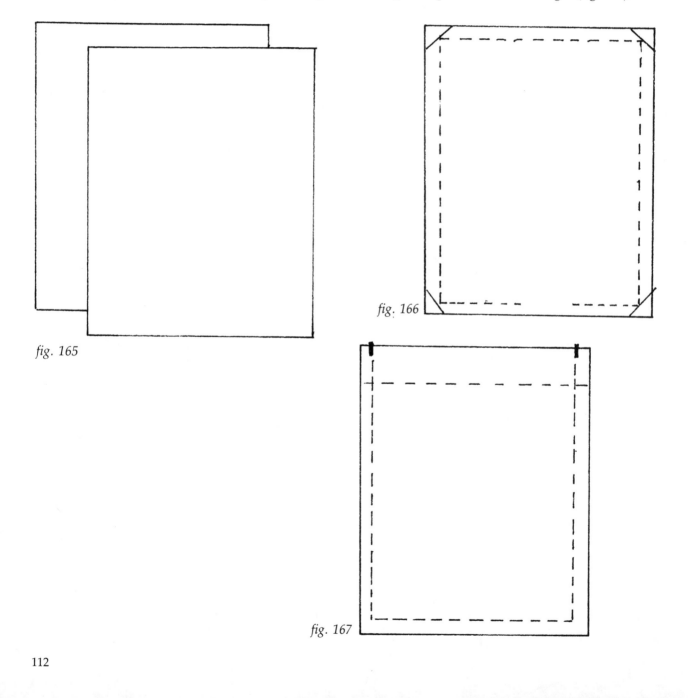

fig. 165

fig. 166

fig. 167

When using heavier fabrics, cut one pocket and allow a 3-inch (7.6-cm) extension at the top for a facing (fig. 168). Iron-on interfacing can be pressed under the flap to give it a little more body. Overcast the raw edge of the flap, fold and stitch at both sides. Sew around the body of the pocket and turn the flap to the right side (fig. 169). Turn the hem allowance under, along the stitching lines. Press firmly. Top-stitch to the garment, ⅛ to ¼ inch (3 to 6 mm) in from the edges, reinforcing at the top (fig. 170).

For a roomier variation, the center of each pocket can be pleated (fig. 171). Add enough width to allow for the pleat (fig. 172). Press pleats and sew around pockets on the stitching line (fig. 173). Fold along the stitching you made and attach to the pants by sewing ⅛ to ¼ inch (3 to 6 mm) in from the edge.

A band can be added at the top, either inside or outside, for greater security (fig. 174). Stitch to the garment, reinforce the top with bartack or backtacking at each side (fig. 175).

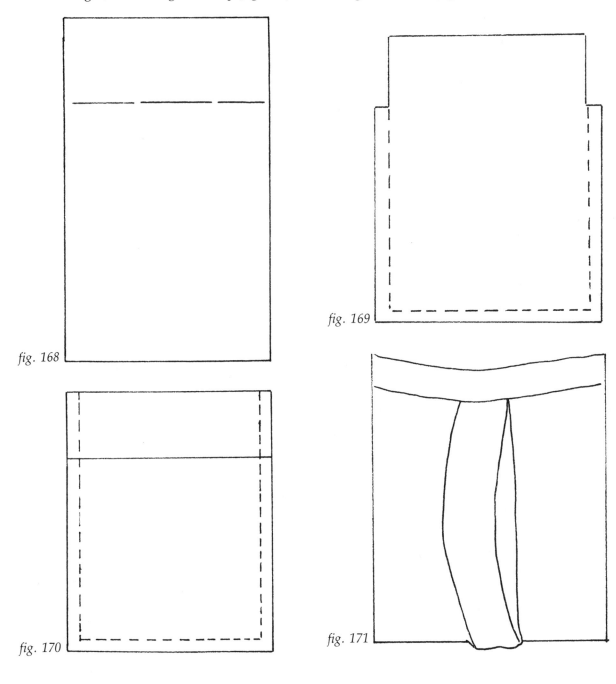

fig. 168

fig. 169

fig. 170

fig. 171

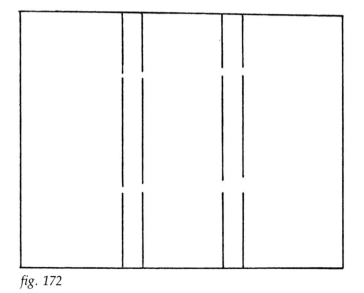

fig. 172

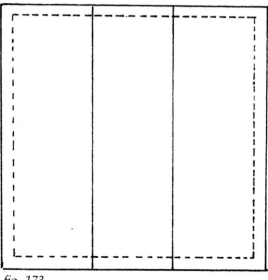

fig. 173

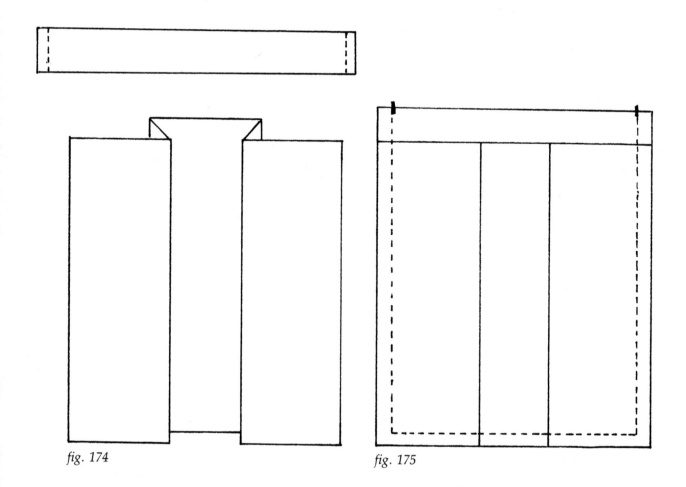

fig. 174

fig. 175

Woven Pants

Put away everything pertaining to the knitted pants pattern. Hang up the slacks you've just finished using and clear the way for your second pants pattern. This one will be fast. You are now familiar with the general system for pants patterns.

Select woven pants that fit you well and look them over (fig. 176).

SURVEY: WOVEN PANTS

A thorough survey of the garment provides information and construction knowledge. As previously noted, it is often simpler to make a pattern from a garment if it is turned inside out (fig. 177). You can see the construction details. Turn your pants and answer the survey questions.

Survey Questions: Woven Pants

1. *Waistband:* What type of waistband is on the garment, elastic or interfaced?
   Elastic: How wide is the elastic? How is it attached?
   Interfaced: How is it interfaced? What type of closure is used?
2. *Pockets:* How many pockets What style? Placement?
3. *Shaping:* Is the top darted or pleated?
4. *Legs:* Are the legs narrow or full? How are they shaped? Is the bottom cuffed or cut straight? Does the crease follow the lengthwise grain? Is it pressed or stitched?
5. *Front/back:* Note the difference between back and front. How much higher is the center back than the side seams at the edges? How much lower is the center front than the side seam edge? How much difference is there between the width of the front and back?

A survey of the woven pants revealed the following information:

- *Shaping:* Trouser style pants with soft pleats at the top. Straight legs, no cuffs.

fig. 176

- *Waistband:* Attached with elastic instead of inter-faced with fabric. Concealed hook under tab, front zipper closure.
- *Pockets:* Inseam pockets at either side of the garment.

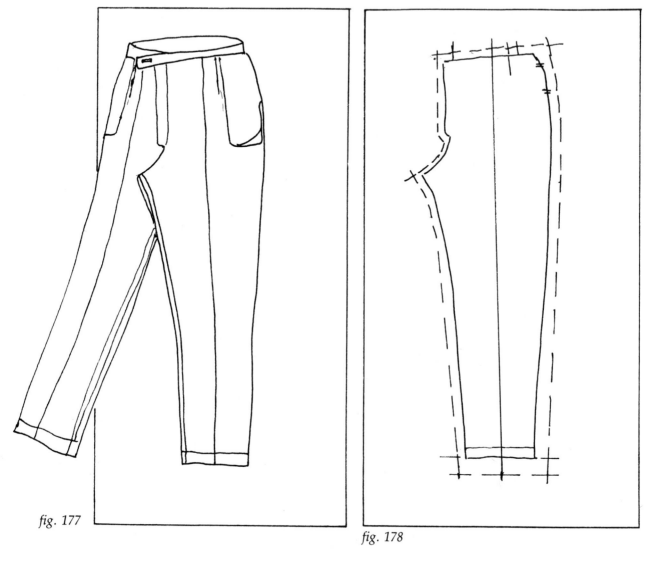

fig. 177

fig. 178

Front

Spread the pants you've chosen on the prepared paper as you did for the knitted pants: front side up, with the excess fabric from the back tucked underneath. Start sketching at the waistline from the center line to the first dart. You can see the amount of fabric included in this dart or pleat so mark the waist for the sewing lines and the edges of the fold (fig. 178). Continue across the waistline to the zipper and mark the installation lines and the extension of the flap. At the outer edge of the pants, add the width of the dart to the waist and taper the line down to meet the existing line from the widest point of the hip.

Follow the contour of the upper hipline curve, including the dart allowance. This is how the shaping is built into a garment made of woven fabric. Continue down the side of the pants to the hem and complete the bottom edge.

Sketch the inseam from the crotch to the bottom of the leg and add the hem facing. If you haven't already folded one leg into the other, do it now and lay the crotch-rise seam on the pattern between the marks. Rough-in the crotch and add the extension for the fold or fly flap (fig. 179). Lift the garment and fold it at the dart to copy the length of this dart onto your pattern.

Mark the length of the zipper on the pattern as well. This will probably be 7½ inches (19.1 cm) which I have never found to be an adequate zipper length. A 9-inch (22.9-cm) zipper for your pants will provide greater access when pulling them on and off.

Remove the garment from the pattern and firm up all lines with contrasting pen. Detail the pattern for future use: date, type of garment—*woven pants* (*front*), size pattern was drafted from, your weight, etc. Set this pattern aside and start the back.

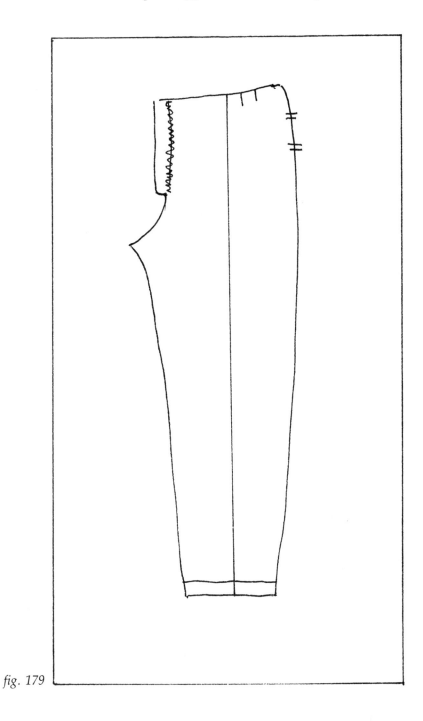

fig. 179

Back

Lay the pants on a fresh sheet of pattern paper and start at the waistline edge as you did for the front. Don't bother to turn them to the right side; the entire pattern can be drafted from the wrong side of the pants. Just turn the waistband inside the garment to expose the top or waistline seam. Mark the back darts, adding the amount of the dart fold to the side seam (fig. 180). Mark the place where the crotch-rise line crosses the waistline. Sketch the outside seam to the bottom of the leg, mark the hem allowance and continue up the inseam of the leg. Mark the point at which the inseam line crosses the crotch line. If the opposite leg has not already been folded into the one you're drawing, do so now and replace the garment on the pattern between the designated marks. Rough-in the crotch-rise line, allowing the shelf to drop below the center or crotch-inseam point. This provides the needed sitting room.

CONSTRUCTION

Most of us have developed our own construction methods when we sew. Maybe it's simple, and maybe it isn't, but it is the method we each know the best. Well, I'm going to ask you to try the following method at least once. It might prove to be the easiest method you have ever used.

Start with the zipper. Lay it face down along the indicated installation line on the right side of the fabric, on the right-hand flap. Yes, the zipper goes in first! Sew along the marked line (fig. 181). Fold the fabric along the stitching line and pull the flap out flat creating a pocket for the zipper tape. Top-stitch about ⅛ inch (3 mm) from the original stitching line (fig. 182). Align the other tape of the zipper for the left side along the fold line, face down (fig. 183). Sew along the indicated line.

Pin the fly fold and secure (preferably with hand stitching, but machine work will do), curving the bottom edge of the sewing line towards the center seam as shown (fig. 184).

Complete the legs of the pants. Sew the rest of the crotch seam together from the center back to the point of the zipper installation. There will be a small gap where you will be unable to get the machine foot completely up to the zipper base. Pick up these few stitches by hand.

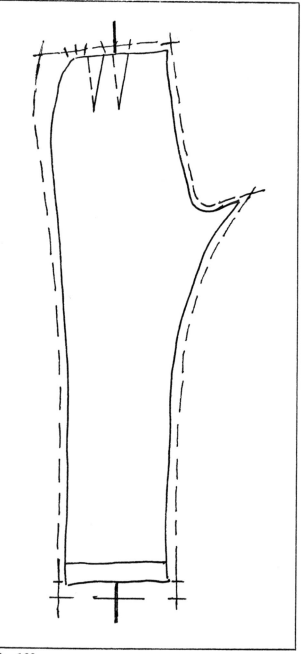

fig. 180

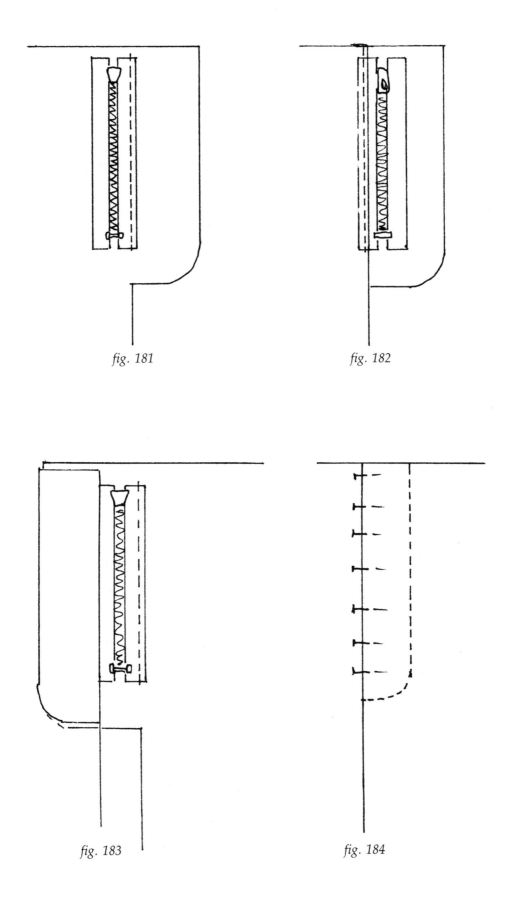

fig. 181

fig. 182

fig. 183

fig. 184

If you feel more confident, try the pants on before you close the outside seams. Any necessary adjustments can be handled from the outside seams.

If you are satisfied with the fit, just sew up the side seams and prepare the waistband to be attached. There are several different approaches to attaching the waistband. The most obvious is to interface the waistband and sew it to the pants. A better method that will give you the waistline fit you've always desired, is to sew the waistband (without any facing) to the pants and cut a piece of elastic 2 to 3 inches (5.1 to 7.6 cm) shorter than the band (fig. 185). Pin it to the ends of the band and place a second pin at each side, just past the points where the button and buttonhole will be applied (fig. 186). Don't stretch the elastic as you do this; you are merely providing a firm base for your button or hook. The elastic will be stretched to fit the space between the second pair of pins inserted into the waistband. Place a pin at the center back of the band, catching the exact center of the elastic. Now pin the center of the remaining elastic at the side seams (fig. 187).

Stitch across the end and past the pin with a slight zigzag stitch, fastening the elastic to the seam edge. From that point, as you stitch, pull the elastic to fit between the pins and stitch in place. Fold the waistband over the elastic and stitch-in-the-ditch for the neatest fitting waistband you've ever put on a pair of pants. Sew the button and buttonhole through the waistband and elastic for a smooth, tailored finish.

The third approach is to apply the waistband in the usual fashion with iron-on interfacing and stitch it to the top of the garment. Before you turn the band, take a piece of elastic 1 to 1½ inches (2.5 to 3.8 cm) shorter than the back half of the waistband and stitch it to the band at the side seam points (fig. 188). Turn the upper part over, and sew the waistband in place, stretching the elastic to fit the back of the band as you stitch-in-the-ditch.

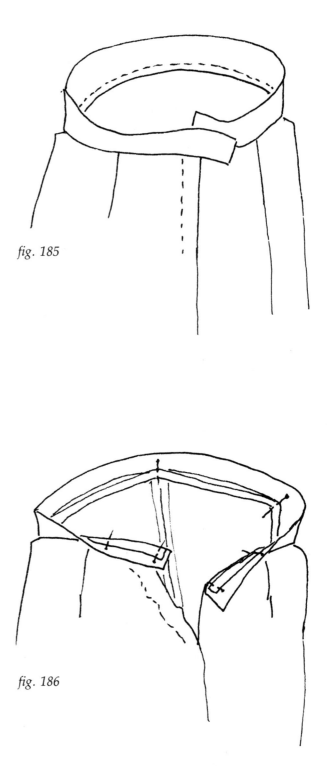

fig. 185

fig. 186

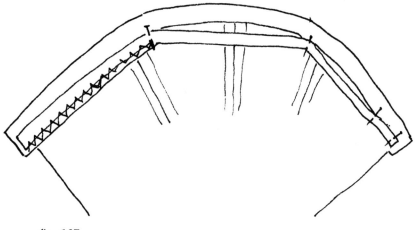

fig. 187

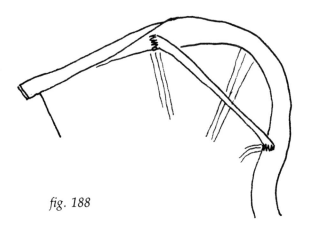

fig. 188

Using Your Pattern Creatively

In the introduction on page 103 I referred to pants styles that can be made from these two basic patterns. We will now perform a little magic and create many styles without making any additional patterns.

Trousers

Trousers are slacks with pleated front and easy legs. Use your basic woven pattern to make a lovely pair of trousers that you will enjoy wearing. The changes are made primarily in the construction of the garment. If the legs of your pants pattern are very fitted, cut them ⅛ inch (3 mm) wider at each seam edge to provide an easier fit. Begin construction with the darts. These will not be stitched down along the sewing line. Instead, create pleats by tucking the amount of the dart at the waistband and stitching across the top (fig. 189). A light pressing will allow the pleat to hang properly. This will give you the trouser-pleat look without any pattern modifications. If you prefer knitted fabric to woven for your trousers, use the knit pattern so that the pants will not be two sizes too big for you. Since the knit pattern is cut straight up from the widest part of the hip, you have the room to create the pleats by folding and stitching the excess fabric as detailed above. The back can be eased into the waistband and will probably still provide enough room for access. If you have trimmed your pattern for a very close fit, cut the garment ¼ inch (6 mm) wider at each side of the top, easing into the regular cutting line at the widest part of the hip (fig. 190). This will

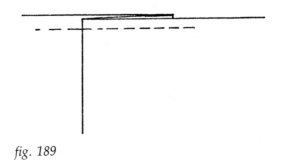

fig. 189

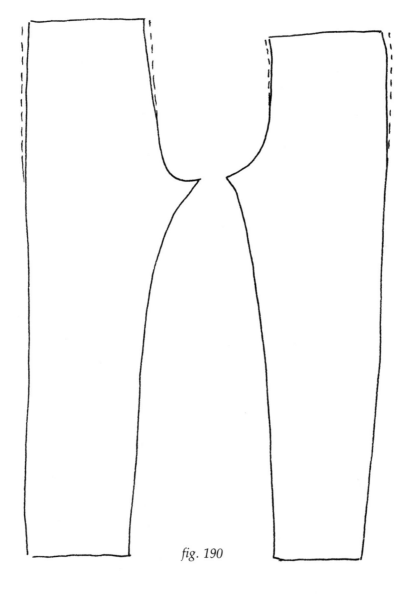

fig. 190

provide pleat room without changing the size of the entire garment. Pleats are then put together just as the original version or with the addition of a zipper, if you prefer. If a zipper is added to the knitted pants, be sure to create a flap for the front of the garment (fig. 191). This can be cut separately and sewn to the front seam. Use seam tape in your stitching line.

If these are to be pull-ons, you can create a false fly by topstitching down the front where you would normally stitch the zipper line. This will create the illusion of a fly front.

Your woven pants pattern might already have pleats indicated at the front. Just sew them in as they were handled on the original garment. If they have front darts, follow the above directions.

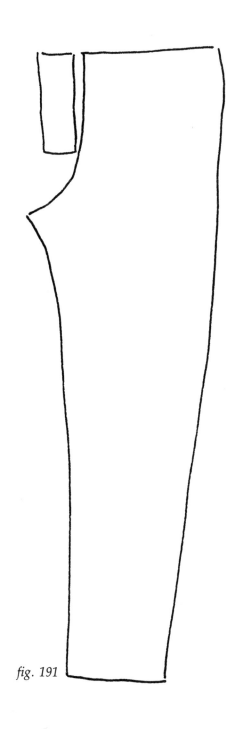

fig. 191

Cropped Pants

Once upon a time pants of this length were called "clam diggers" (fig. 192). Any type of straight-legged pants can be cut or cropped to the current fashion. The hem could be 1 inch (2.5 cm) above the ankle or mid-shin. The pants legs should be widened at least an inch or two to hang properly. Add half the amount of width you choose to each side of the leg, both front and back. Taper the new cutting line to meet the original line of the pattern.

Wrap Pants

There are several versions of *wrap pants*. The first is wrap-waistband pants (fig. 193). The waistband is cut like a scarf, 16 inches to 20 inches wide (40.6 to 50.8 cm) by approximately 60 inches (152.4 cm) long. It is centered at the waist, either front or back, depending upon the closure of the pants (fig. 194). When it is attached, it can either be worn as a sashed waist or pulled up over the bosom and wrapped around the upper body like a bandeau. Either way is very attractive and versatile, changing the look from pants to jumpsuit. This type of waistband lends itself beautifully to palazzo pants.

In another version of *wrap pants* there is an extension at both sides of the fly front, creating an overlap on the front (fig. 195). The waistband extensions can meet rings at the sides or wrap completely around, meeting a buckle at the front (fig. 196). With this style, you might use a couple of small pieces of Velcro fastening tape as a closure, instead of a zipper; or you can attach grip fasteners down the diagonal front (fig. 197). You can also make the pants from the regular pattern and extend the waistband to belt length at the ends (fig. 198). It will wrap completely around the waist in opposite directions and meet at a buckle. Very nice look.

fig. 192

fig. 193

fig. 194

fig. 195

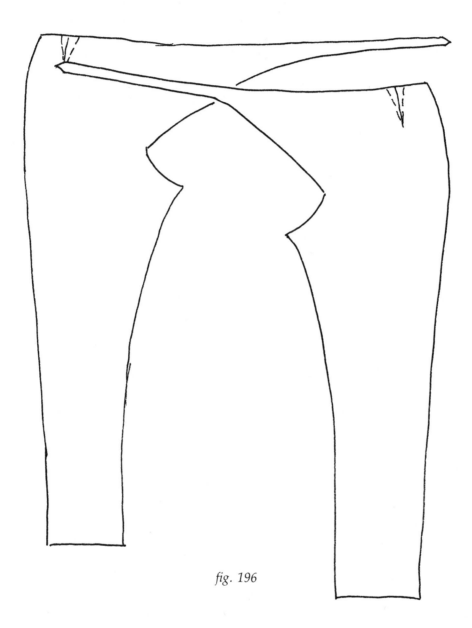

fig. 196

fig. 197

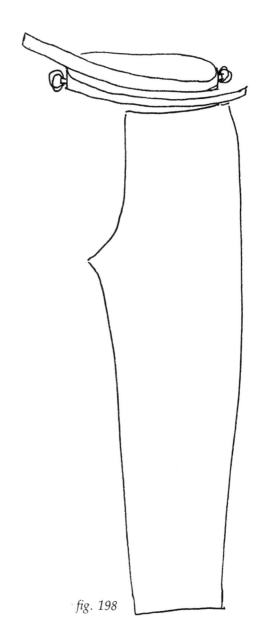

fig. 198

Palazzo Pants

I have mentioned palazzo pants in earlier paragraphs. These are wonderful pants that can go from the patio to the dance floor and look at home in both places (fig. 199), a style that is kind to most figures and is very comfortable. With your own sloper you will be able to create these wonderful pants in a proportion that will flatter your figure. Nylon tricot, Qiana nylon or other soft, flowing fabric will work well with this style. You can cut directly from a pair of pants or from your pattern.

Most of these soft knits come in 60-inch (152.4-cm) widths; you will need 2 lengths to accommodate your pattern. Since you will be working with so much fabric, you might want to work on the floor. Lay the fabric out, so that you won't have to

fig. 199

move it around too much. When planning this type of garment, I like to allow about 2 to 3 inches (5.1 to 7.6 cm) beyond the width of the pattern for gathering or pleating. Fold the fabric lengthwise placing the outside edge of the pants parallel to the fold and 2 to 3 inches (5.1 to 7.6 cm) from it. Because of the width of these pants there is no need for side seams (fig. 200). The pleats or gathers will take care of the hip shaping. Allow only 1 inch (2.5 cm) for a shal-

low hem at the bottom. You can hem these pants on the machine.

Cut across the top of the pattern following the waistline (fig. 201). Cut the crotch-rise line but allow an extra inch in the crotch. Then cut straight down to the hem. Do not shape the vertical seam lines. These pants are as full as a skirt and should hang straight to the floor. Cut the other half of the pattern.

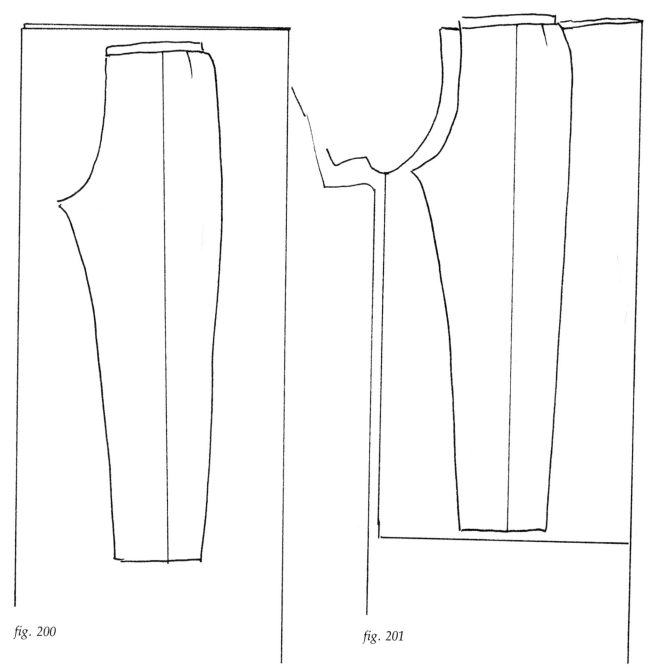

fig. 200

fig. 201

If you are adding pockets, slit the side on the fold and insert them at each side seam (see Inseam Pockets, page 32). Sew the garment from the hem to the waist for the smoothest seam finish. Be sure you are sewing a front and back for each leg. To identify garment segments: use small pieces of masking tape and label them *front* and *back*. When the sections are cut, press a piece of tape to the appropriate piece and you will always have the fronts and backs sewn together properly.

When the seam of each leg has been completed, turn one leg inside out and place the right-side-out leg inside the one you reversed. Sew the crotch seam in one sweep, from the front, around through the inseam point (reinforce where the seams cross) and up the back. Cut the usual amount of elastic 2 inches (5.1 cm) less than your actual waistline measurement), and wrap it around the garment when you try it on to assure the crotch fit. Attach the waistband. Finish the hem by either topstitching or blind-hemming on your sewing machine.

If you would rather have a separate pattern for palazzo pants, you can draft one from any pants or pants pattern that fits you. Follow the same general directions, allowing 2 to 3 inches (5.1 to 7.6 cm) at the outer edge and ½ to 1 inch (1.3 to 2.5 cm) at the inseam while following the crotch-rise line exactly. For added fullness, swing the bottom edge out approximately 2 inches (5.1 cm) from center on the outside seam only. The inseam line should still fall straight to prevent the pants from bunching in the crotch and inseam as you walk.

Drawstrings

Using your basic pants pattern, cut drawstring pants straight up from the widest part of the hip to the waistline (fig. 202). This is similar to the knitted pants. Shape the legs in the same manner as the pattern. Since drawstring pants are large at the top, you can dispense with the zipper for the woven pattern (fig. 203). These can be pulled on and snugged in at the waist to complete the fit. The construction is the same as any other pants. Sew an eyelet at the center of the waistband to admit the drawstring. The waistband won't need any interfacing unless your fabric is very thin. If you prefer a zipper, attach it as you did for the original pair of pants.

fig. 202

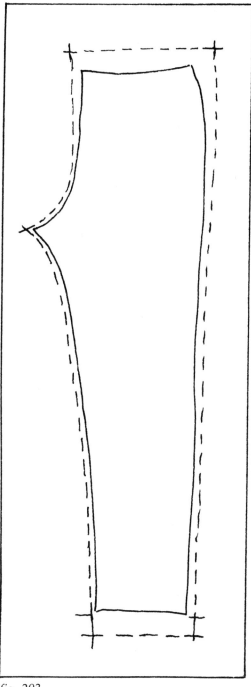

fig. 203

Sweat Pants

Sweat pants are wonderful (fig. 204). They have all the comforts built in—knit fabric, loose fit, pull-on, elastic or drawstring waist, knitted cuffs and pockets. I make these pants in many colors and have declared them my work uniform. Sitting at the typewriter for hours at a time couldn't be more comfortable than in brightly colored sweat pants.

Always preshrink sweat-shirt fabric. It can have some rather erratic properties. I had one batch of fabric shrink on the bias. Needless to say, it went back to the shop.

fig. 204

Use your knit pants pattern to cut your warm-ups. Add about ¼ inch (6 mm) to the outside edges as you cut, for comfort, if you like them baggy (fig. 205). Eliminate the hem allowance if you are adding ribbing to the bottom of the leg, cutting along the fold line of the hem. The full amount of the hem facing will make the legs too long.

Cut them out, stitch them together with a serging stitch on your machine (or if you own an overlock machine, use it for the entire garment). Cut the top long enough to fold over as a waistband, instead of cutting it as a separate piece. Saves time and effort.

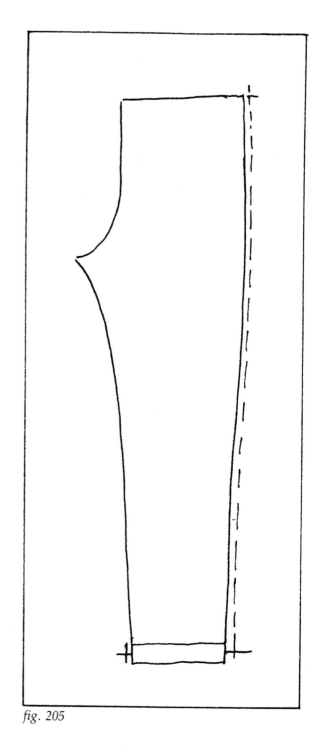

fig. 205

Athletic Shorts

These brief shorts are slit at the sides or cut up round the bend at the top of the leg for additional comfort. The general directions are the same. Since we just discussed sweat pants, I'll begin with some information about athletic shorts (fig. 206). Runners, joggers, aerobic dancers and others seem to like to wear these brief pants over their warm-ups. You can easily cut them from leftover fabric from your sweat suits.

Use the pattern you drafted for *knit pants*, already adjusted to fit you. Mark the inseam line 1½ inches (3.8 cm) below the crotch point (fig. 207). Mark the outside seam line at the point just below your buttocks. For a side slit, to give additional comfort, allow 2 inches (5.1 cm) for an opening at the side seam. Connect these points. Do not cut your pattern. You will fold the leg under when you cut the shorts. Mark the back of the pattern in the same manner.

Short Shorts

These little gems are very flattering to long, slim legs (fig. 208). They are also a joy to make, because you can run them up on the sewing machine in no time. Your woven fabric pants pattern will need a few additional adjustments to cut these shorts.

The inseam line should be marked at a point approximately 2 inches (5.1 cm) below the crotch line (fig. 209). Use a T square to bring the line across the pattern and cross the outside seam. When this pattern is cut, extend the outside line of the leg out approximately ½ inch (1.3 cm) at each side. Taper the line up to meet the existing cutting line. This will allow a little extra room at the lower edge of the shorts to keep the hem hanging straight at the bottom and prevent it from pulling in towards the leg. Allow at least 1½ inches (3.8 cm) for the hem.

Jamaicas

The cutting lines for these shorts are also added to your woven pants pattern (fig. 210). Jamaicas are usually half the distance between the bend at the

fig. 206

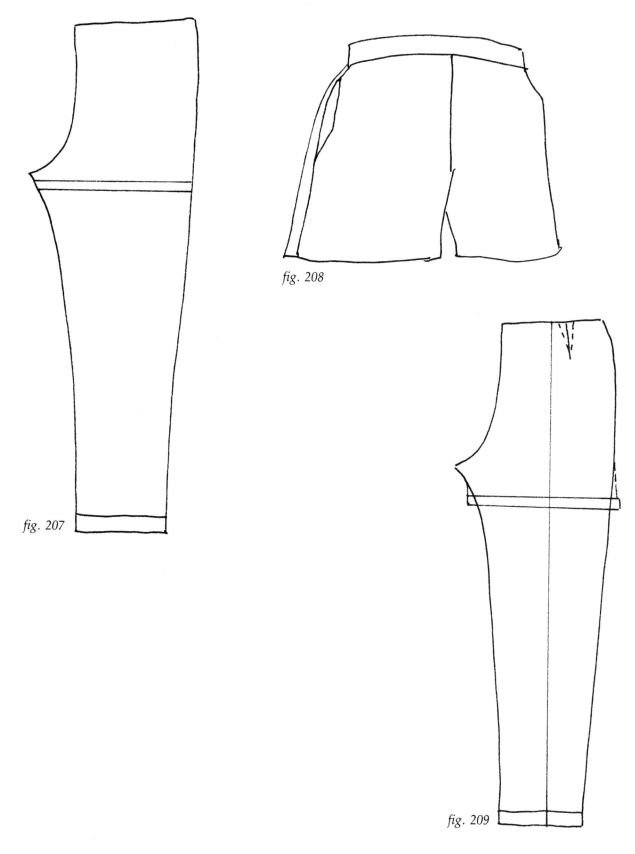

fig. 207

fig. 208

fig. 209

top of the leg and the top of the knee. Measure your own leg or an existing pair of Jamaicas that you find comfortable, and mark the length on your pants pattern.

Repeat the ease adjustment for the bottom edge as it is detailed in the section on Short Shorts. Adding this hemline ease is even more crucial for the longer shorts because they are tapered.

Bermudas

Bermudas are the most modest length for shorts (fig. 211), approximately 1½ inches (3.8 cm) above the bend at the back of the knee, according to some earlier golfing dress codes. Bermudas are a good compromise between long pants and short shorts. One to 1½ inches (2.5 to 3.8 cm) above the kneecap is a pretty good measure for the length of these pants. They look particularly good when made from madras cotton or twill for summer, gabardine or corduroy for winter.

fig. 210

Culottes

This comfortable combination of pants and skirt can truly "go anywhere" today (fig. 212). Culottes are as versatile at knee length as they are at shinbone length. Whatever the season, whatever the occasion, these pants can be worn in place of a skirt—that's the image they present.

Culottes make up beautifully in either woven or knitted fabrics. The following instructions refer to wovens but the same directions apply to knits as well.

Lay the fabric out on your cutting table and place the *front* pants pattern face up, with the widest part of the hipline curve inside the selvage. Measure your chosen length on the pattern and draw a line across the leg at that point (fig. 213). (Don't forget to allow for the hem facing.) Fold the excess length under, and hold it in place with a couple of pins. Put a weight on your pattern and start by cutting the top of the garment. Cut the shaping of the side to the widest part of the hip (fig. 214). From there, cut straight down to the hemline. Cut the curve of the crotch line and 1 inch (2.5 cm) of the inseam. Continue straight down to the hemline from that point.

fig. 211

fig. 212

Cut across the bottom edge of the garment. You have completed cutting the front.

To cut the *back*, follow the above directions. Always cut straight down from the widest part of the hip for a proper hang to the garment. When you've marked the length for these culottes on the pattern, you will have a permanent record of this length for your convenience.

The above directions, used for 12- to 14-inch (30.5- to 35.6-cm) culottes will give you a nice tennis pants/skirt. Made up in a 16- to 18-inch length (40.6- to 45.7-cm) the culottes would be practical and enjoyable for golf.

We have now gone full circle. Your two pants patterns are capable of yielding an unlimited number of lengths and styles.

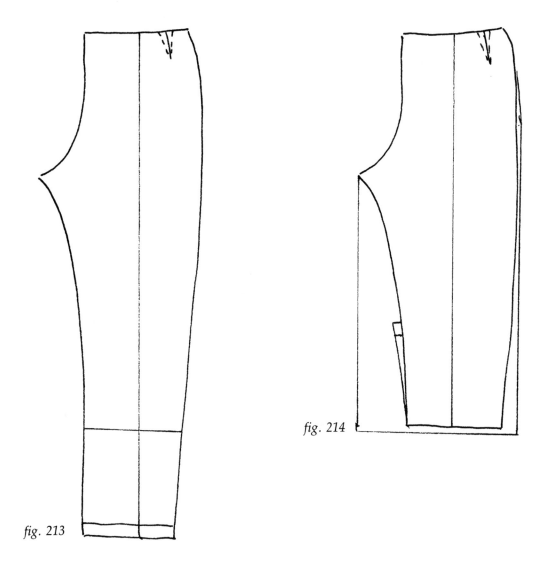

fig. 213

fig. 214

fig. 215

THE ULTIMATE PATTERN

Rousing book finishes always make me want to go back to the beginning of the book, because I hate to see the story end. I hope this chapter will inspire the same feeling in you.

The chapter title is not an extravagance of words; the ultimate pattern already exists in your pattern file, if you have been working along with each chapter in this book. The ultimate pattern is the combination of unrelated pieces from your personal patterns.

All pieces from the patterns you make for yourself are interchangeable, and everything in your wardrobe is a potential pattern. The only limitations are your imagination, daring and willingness to try something new.

Having extremely long legs, I rarely find a ready-made dress with enough skirt length to please me. When I started to sew, I tried to adjust commercial patterns by adding several inches below the hem. This occasionally had disastrous effects on the basic lines of the design. Stubbornly using my method of trial and error, I developed a workable system for making dresses with no doubt about the results. They're perfect every time.

Dresses

I start with a plan for a design that will suit me. I collect the components from pattern pieces and existing garments and go to work. Combine the body of a blouse with the sleeve from your favorite sweat shirt, the pattern for a comfortable skirt, and you've assembled the parts for a lovely dress for that party next weekend (fig. 215). Make a sketch of the finished garment. You will always know how the pieces are supposed to go together when you plan it yourself and work from your own sketch.

To make your new style, cut directly from the assemblage or draft a pattern. Either way works. Always start by cutting the largest pieces first. The small ones can be cut from scraps or ends of the fabric. Cut the skirt, the bodice and the sleeves (fig. 216). Cut the facings last. If you end up with some rather large scraps, try to piece together a scarf; it will change the look of the neckline and protect your shoulders from drafts. Cut belts from the selvages, using the woven end as the seam allowance.

TENT DRESS

Let's assemble a few pattern pieces, and create a lovely tent dress (fig. 217). The sleeveless top pattern has enough ease built into it to cut from woven fabric without any changes. Fold the top pattern at the waistline casing and butt the A-line skirt pattern up against the fold, matching the outside lines. Cut straight down the outside line. Try a tulip or belled sleeve with this style and use the cowl collar. The dress should go together in record-breaking time and could be a great favorite as it will wash well (if you preshrink your fabric first).

fig. 216

fig. 217

SHIRTWAIST DRESS

This is practically an eternal style. It is probably the only style that is still as popular today as when it first came out (fig. 218). I detailed a shirtwaist dress (page 59) that shows how to extend the lines to dress length. There are other styles for the shirtwaist pattern.

Combining the blouse with the A-line skirt pattern (page 87) results in a softly flared shirtwaist (fig. 219). By using the straight skirt pattern, adding 2 to 3 inches (5.1 to 7.6 cm) to the front and back width, you create a skirt with unpressed pleats, a softer look than the straight version (fig. 220). With either of these versions, elastic can be used at the waistline for a snug fit. Or make the dress with a drawstring and casing—you won't have to worry about a belt.

fig. 218

fig. 219

fig. 220

Jumpsuit

If you've never owned a jumpsuit you've missed one of the most versatile and comfortable garments ever designed. But the jumpsuit presents even more problems than the dress. It is not only difficult to buy, it is a devil to make. When commercially made, the jumpsuit fits very few people. The most common problem is the length from shoulder to crotch, forcing the wearer to stoop over a lot. If you have been lucky enough to find a jumpsuit that did fit, then you know what a comfortable and versatile item this can be. If you haven't ever owned a jumpsuit, this is your moment. You now have the components in your pattern file for your jumpsuit with a perfect fit. You'll enjoy making it, but more, wearing it will be an absolute treat.

JUMPSUIT: KNIT FABRICS

We will start with one of the *top* patterns we drafted from knit fabric (page 25). Combining this with the pattern for knit pants, we will create an entirely new and exciting garment (fig. 221).

fig. 221

With a knit jumpsuit you have the option of creating a step-in style without closures (fig. 222). It can be shaped with the addition of elastic at the waist and neckline to allow enough room to pull it up over the hips. If you think the garment might be worn without a belt, and you like the balloon shape, you can eliminate the elastic at the waistline. This simple jumpsuit can be done completely on the sewing machine (including hems) and be ready to wear in about two hours.

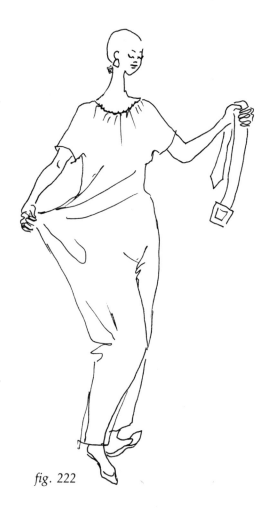

fig. 222

Let's get down to some serious work. You will have to decide whether you want a seam down the center back and front or whether you would prefer a waistline seam. With a seam at the waist, the top is cut in one piece, and the lower section is cut separately. With the center-front seam, the entire front (top and pants) is cut in two sections (fig. 223).

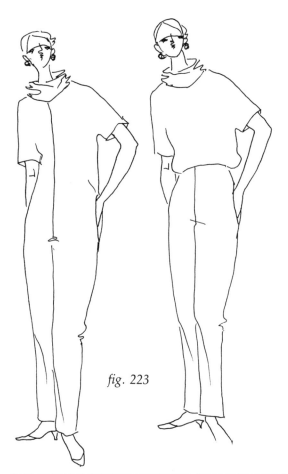

fig. 223

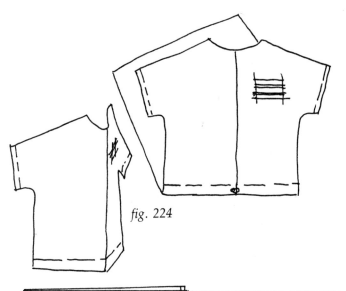

fig. 224

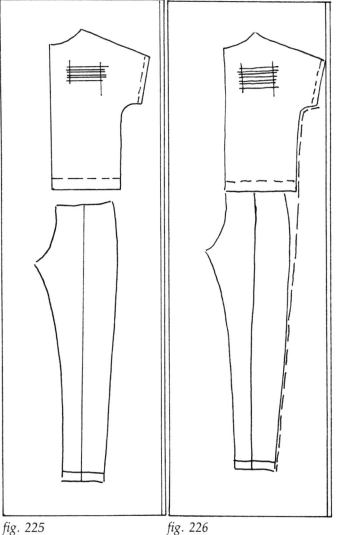

fig. 225   fig. 226

JUMPSUIT WITH CENTER-FRONT SEAM

Starting with the *top front* of the pattern, fold this section of the bodice along the casing line. This is where the blouse and pants sections will be joined. Then fold it in half vertically along the center front line (fig. 224). Place this quarter section on the fabric at the top, with the capped sleeve near the selvage and the center front near the fold of the fabric. Allow enough room for the entire crotch section to fit on the fabric. Butt the *front* section of the pants against the top, matching the waistline of the pants to the casing line of the top (fig. 225). The *center* lines of both pattern pieces should be parallel to the selvages of the fabric. Pin the two pattern sections together along the waistline, or put weights on them to hold them in place while you cut. The outside lines of the two pattern pieces probably will not meet, but as you cut the outside seam line, you will adjust these lines with your scissors creating one smooth, straight line from the underarm to the bottom of the leg (fig. 226). Repeat the same procedure for the *back*.

JUMPSUIT WITH WAISTLINE SEAM

If you choose not to have a center seam, cut the top in the conventional manner. Place the front and back of the bodice on the fold of the fabric. Add a seam allowance below the casing line where the pattern is folded under (fig. 227). Include all seam allowances when you cut the pants. When a jumpsuit with waistline seam is sewn together, start with the center-front seams of the pants, then attach the bottom to the top at the waistline. Sew the center-back seam of the pants and attach the bodice and bottoms. When the shoulder seams are sewn, try

on the jumpsuit and make necessary adjustments at the open side seams. Stitch the side seams in one continuous line from bottom to top.

If you are planning an elastic casing for the neckline, you won't need any facings for the neck edge (fig. 228). Either cut a separate casing which can be attached to the neck edge, or turn the top of the garment as you sew, creating a casing of the same fabric. If you planned inseam pockets, sew these in now, before the side seams are sewn together. Sew the outside seams from bottom to top. Complete the shoulder seams. Sew the inseam of the suit in one continuous line up one side and down the other.

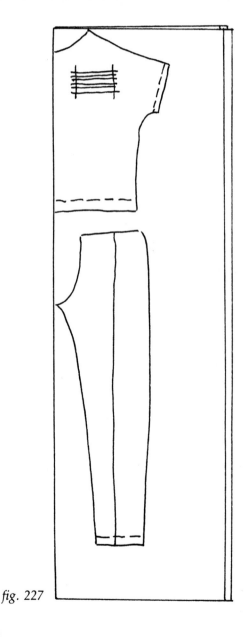

fig. 227

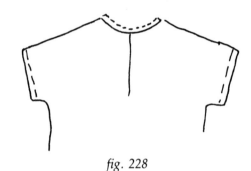

fig. 228

Put in your hem by machine after you try the garment on and check the length.

To finish the neck edge, sew the casing and thread elastic through it (or make an elastic ring and sew the casing over the elastic).

There are many ways to style a jumpsuit. You can add a drawstring at the neckline and/or the waistline (fig. 229) instead of the elastic. You might prefer a keyhole opening at the neckline. This is a smoother, possibly dressier, look (fig. 230). For this style, you will have to create a facing for the neckline. After you design the size and shape of your keyhole opening, lay the top of the garment on either the fabric or pattern paper and draw the neck opening for the front and back (fig. 231). Allow 2½ to 3 inches (6.4 to 7.6 cm) at the narrowest point for a smoother facing. The pattern piece can be made long enough to include the entire opening.

As you sew the facing in, add a piece of seam tape along the neck edge between the facing and bodice. This will prevent the top from stretching. The neckline can be secured with a decorative button, a snap or ties. Just be sure when creating this type of neckline opening that it will admit your hips. A jumpsuit is, after all, a step-in garment.

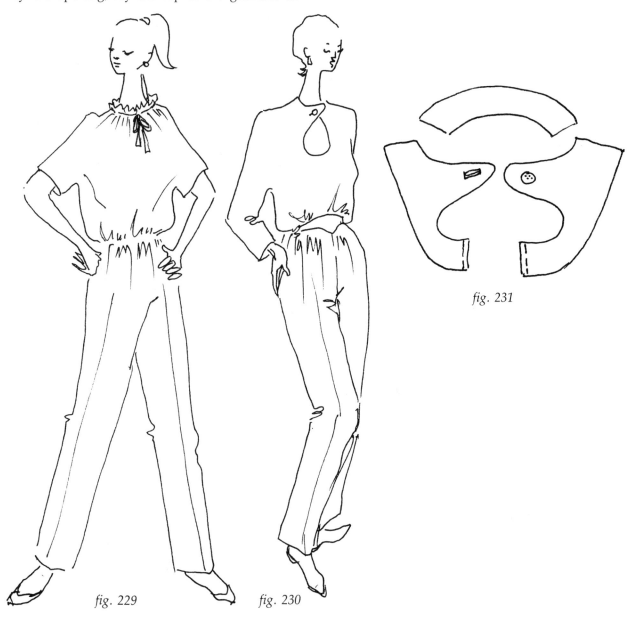

fig. 229   fig. 230

fig. 231

JUMPSUIT: WOVEN FABRIC

Woven fabrics make a big difference in the jumpsuit's styling. Closures *must* be planned since woven fabrics don't have enough built-in ease to admit the body to a step-in garment. Decide on the type of closure to be used: buttons, zipper, snaps, etc. (fig. 232). Will a placket be added as a separate piece or cut in one piece with the front? Maybe you prefer grip fasteners.

Your jumpsuit could have an opening at the shoulders, using buttons, Velcro fastening tape or snaps, instead of opening down the front (fig. 233). This creates a totally new, uncluttered look—a perfect foil for jewelry.

Using the second pattern we drafted, the top with sleeves from woven fabric (page 45), and adding the pattern for woven pants (page 115), we have our jumpsuit pattern. Again, you will have to decide if you want the waistline seam or just the opening down the front (fig. 234). The shirt pattern already includes the placket for the front of the bodice; this will just be extended approximately 8 inches (20.3 cm) down the front, into the pants section. The bodice section can then be closed in a different manner than the pants section. Buttons or snaps

fig. 232

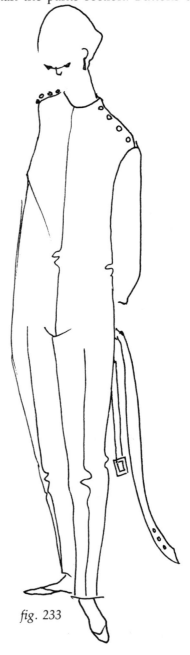

fig. 233

fig. 234

can be used for the top, and a zipper installed in the bottom, starting from the waistline.

Fold the front of the shirt pattern at the waistline and pin it to the waistline of the pants pattern (fig. 235). If the top is to be a blouson style, allow 2 to 3 inches (5.1 to 7.6 cm) at the waist for fold-over. Cut a left and right half for the front. The placket and facing will be cut as one long strip that will go from the neckline to the curve of the crotch (fig. 236).

The back of the top can be cut in one piece even if the front has two pieces. Fold the pattern piece at the waist, add the blousing as you did for the front and cut the back of the bodice (fig. 237). To eliminate the waistline seam at the back, match the top and bottom patterns at the waist. Cut the combined patterns on the folded fabric to make a left and right back section.

A mandarin collar is nice for this style (fig. 238). Measure the neck opening and cut a straight piece of fabric the same length by 3 inches (7.6 cm) wide. Use iron-on interfacing to hold the collar shape. Fold the collar in half lengthwise and attach at the neck.

Your jumpsuit can also be made without sleeves (fig. 239). To make the necessary facing, be sure that the armhole is the right depth. Trace the shape of the front armhole opening and indicate the shoulder line. Align the back of the armhole opening with these lines. Trace the other half of the opening. Allowing about 2¼ inches (5.7 cm) beyond this rough outline, follow your original drawing and create the outside of the shape (fig. 240). This will give you a facing with enough width to include a simple turned hem. Your closure should coordinate

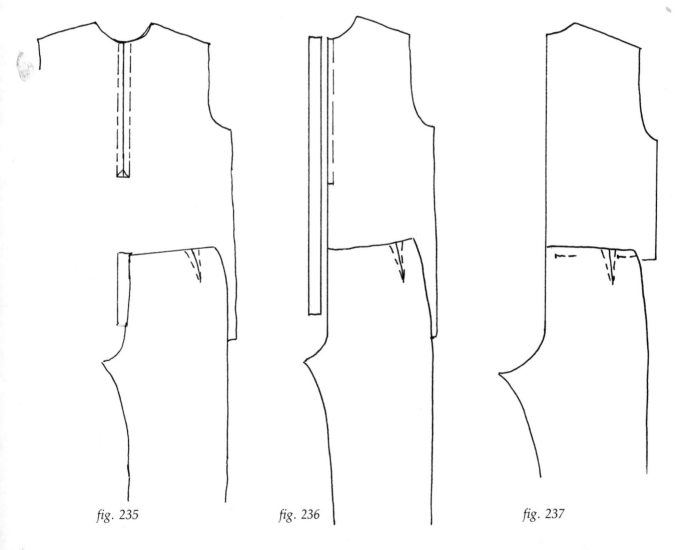

fig. 235   fig. 236   fig. 237

152

and make a personal statement at the same time. Choose *buttons* carefully. They really make or break a garment. For sportswear, consider wooden or bone buttons. Many local potters have been turning out handmade porcelain buttons that are very at-tractive and unusual. Grip fasteners don't have to look like they're leftovers from children's sewing. There are colored or jewelled snaps, many new sizes in metal and even industrial grippers with logos that are very handsome.

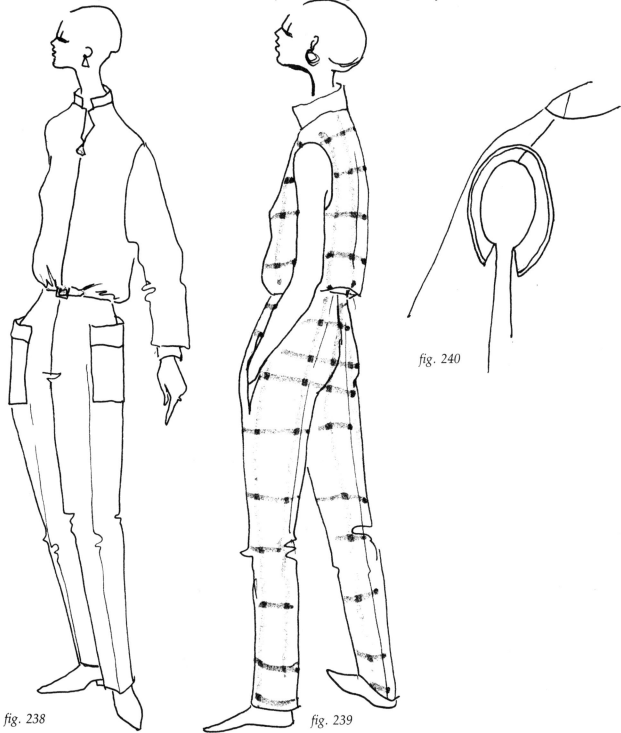

fig. 240

fig. 238

fig. 239

Embroidery or appliqué can turn a simple jump-suit into an elegant outfit (fig. 241). Machine embroidery is fast and attractive. Embroider a nursery rhyme or bit of poetry up one sleeve and down the other. Appliqué or embroider waves on both cuffs (fig. 242). Embroider boats and fish on the legs of the pants and birds on the sleeves, carrying the theme up to the top. There are so many ways to decorate a jumpsuit. Have fun with it. Be inventive, a little wild.

BIB OVERALLS

Bib overalls, a form of jumpsuit, have become quite popular with the young set (fig. 243). They are easy to create by adding a rectangle approximately 7 by 9 inches (17.8 to 22.9 cm), to the center front of the pants section. Long straps are sewn to the back waistline, 2 to 3 inches (5.1 to 7.6 cm) on each side of the center-back seam. The straps can be attached at the waistband, crossed in back and snapped or buttoned to the bib in front. The garment opening should be at either the side or the back.

More Ideas

Make a jumpsuit of sweat-shirt fabric and wear it with different belts to suit the occasion. A belt of bright-colored webbing with matching sandals can go to lunch or the supermarket while a jewelled belt with high-heeled sandals will dress the same jump-suit for an evening of dancing (fig. 244). Versatile jumpsuits are acceptable for almost any occasion, anywhere. And for a quick getaway, they certainly save time when packing.

You can use your knit pants pattern and combine it with the original pattern for the sleeveless top or you can lay out a comfortable sweat suit and use it for the pattern. Either way will work well adding comfort and originality to your wardrobe.

You have now reached the bottom line on the system for drafting patterns from finished clothes. By creating your first simple pattern, your approach to sewing takes a new direction. The door to the world of fashion opens on a more personal level than ever before. What your eyes see or your heart desires, your hands create.

fig. 241

This book is designed to serve as a reference long after the basic system becomes part of your sewing skills. Use it continuously to draft patterns and design new items from existing garments with confidence that everything you make will fit. This book is your teacher, helping you expand on the original system. Use it creatively and pleasurably.

fig. 242

fig. 243

fig. 244

INDEX

A

A-line style
   shirtwaist dresses, 145
   skirts, 11, 35, 78, 87
Alterations, 98
Appliqué, 101
Armhole(s)
   curves, 46
   facings, 152
   openings, 47, 48
Athletic shorts, 136
At-home clothing, 42, 59

B

Backing, skirt, 78
Back of pattern
   garment with capped sleeves, 27–29
   garment with set-in sleeves, 46–47
   knit pants, 108–109
   skirts, 71
   woven pants, 118–121
Bandeau, 124
Belts, 154
Bermuda shorts, 138
Bib overalls, 154
Blouson style, 16
Buckles, 125
Buttonholes for drawstrings, 30
Buttons, 150, 153

C

Capped-sleeved garments
   back of pattern, 27–29
   front of pattern, 30–32
   pockets, 32–35
   survey questions, 25
   variations of, 34–44
Casings
   drawstring, 25, 34
   elastic, 148
Center back line, 28
Center front seam, jumpsuit with, 147
"Clam diggers," 124
Closures
   buttons, 150, 151, 153

grip fasteners, 124, 150, 153
   snaps, 150, 151
   Velcro fastening tape, 124, 150
   zippers, 117–119, 123, 150
Coats, 56, 58
Coding of pattern pieces, 29, 34
   for collars, 56
   for pants, 107, 109, 117
   for sleeves, 47, 48, 54
Collars
   cowl, 25, 34, 143
   curved, 45, 55–56
   direct cutting of, 34
   mandarin, 152, 153
Color, 9, 14
Commercial patterns
   armhole openings, 47
   comparison with drafted patterns, 51, 54
   envelopes, 7
   pieces, 28
   seam allowances, 26
Cotton, 9
Cowl collars, 25, 34, 143
Cropped pants, 124
Crotch of pants, 103, 107, 117
Cuffs, sleeve, 45
Culottes, 139–141
Curved hems, 93
Curved lines, 11
Cutting lines, 27, 47, 107
Cutting without patterns, 34, 61

D

Darts
   on pants, 117, 118
   on skirts, 72–73, 75
   readjusting, 70, 99
Denim skirts, 64
Diagonal lines, 12
Direct-cut method, 61
Dirndl skirts, 62, 88–89, 102
Drafting materials for patterns, 7
Drawstrings, 24, 30–32, 56
   direct cutting of, 34
   neckline, 149

pants, 132–133
skirts, 102
waist for jumpsuits, 149
Dresses
ankle length, 34–38
panels, 13
from shirt patterns, 59
shirtwaist, 16, 145
tent, 16, 143, 144
tunic, 25–34
Dry cleaning, 15

E
Edge-linings, 59
Elastic
necklines, 148
waistbands, 109, 120–121
Embroidery, 101, 102, 154, 155
machine stitches, 40
Empire lines, 11
Envelopes, pattern, 7–8
Equipment, pattern-drafting, 7
Eyelets, drawstring, 30, 31, 32

F
Fabrics. *See also* specific type of fabric
care of, 15
clingy, 14
colors, 14
knitted, 103
plaid, 28
seasonality of, 9
textures, 14–15
woven, 45
Facings
armhole, 152, 153
neckline, 149
skirt, 74
Fashions, 9–13
Figure types, 9
half-size, 22
heavy thighs, 100
hip-heavy, 21–22
queen-size, 22
short and heavy, 18
short and slim, 16–17
tall and heavy, 19
top heavy, 20–21
Filing cabinets, as pattern organizers, 7
Filing of patterns, 8
Flannel, 40
Fly front
extension of, 124, 125
false, 123
flap, 117–119
skirt, 76

Front of pattern
garment with cap sleeves, 30–31
garment with set-in sleeves, 45, 48
knit pants, 106–107
skirt, 74–77
woven pants, 116–117
Fur fabrics, 15

G
Godets, 98
Golf skirts, 101, 102
Gored skirts, 62, 95
Grain lines, importance of, 28, 79, 106
Grip fasteners, 124, 129, 150, 153

H
Hand-hemming, 32
Handkerchief hemlines, 94
Hem allowances, 27, 29, 47
Hemline(s)
curved, 93
handkerchief, 94
length, 40
shirttail, 39, 41
Hemming, 32, 38
Hip-waist proportions, 99
Hoods on loungeware, 42, 43
Horizontal lines, 11

I
Inseam pockets, 26, 32, 33, 34, 111
Instructions. *See* Coding of pattern pieces
Interfacing, 113, 120, 121, 152
Ironing of pattern pieces, 8

J
Jackets, pullover, 56, 58
Jamaica shorts, 136, 137, 138
Jumpsuits
bib overall, 154, 155
knit fabric, 146–149
woven fabric, 150–156

K
Keyhole opening neckline, 149
Knitted fabrics, 103
cotton single knit, 111
jumpsuits from, 146–149
pants from, 106–114

L
Layout of pattern, 26
Length(s)
adjustment, 66, 98
dress, 37
skirt, 27, 29
Lines, garment, 10–13. *See also* specific lines
Lining

pocket, 112
skirt, 79

M
Mandarin collars, 152, 153
Markings, pattern, 27–30, 47–48

N
Necklines
  boat, 26
  drafting, 28, 47
  drawstring, 149
  elasting casing for, 148
  facing, 31
  keyhole opening, 149
  variations, 36, 40
Nightgowns, 39–41
Nonwoven textiles, 7
Notes, on pattern pieces. *See* Coding of pattern pieces
Nylon, 56, 130

O
On-fold line, 28
Organization, of sewing room, 7–8
Overalls, bib, 154, 155
Overlock stitching, 111

P
Palazzo pants, 130–132
Pants. *See also* Culottes, Shorts
  back, drafting, 108–109, 118–120
  construction of, 110–111
  cropped, 124
  drawstrings, 132–133
  fitting, 103–104
  front, drafting, 106–107, 116–117
  knit, 104–111
  patch pockets for, 112–114
  pleated, 122–123
  pull-on, 41
  survey questions, 104, 115
  sweat, 134–135
  trousers, 122–123
  variations, 120
  woven, 115–120
  wrap, 124–129
Patch pockets, 40, 101, 112–113
Patchwork garments, 102
Pattern paper
  for shirts, 46, 49
  for skirts, 71
  preparing, 27
  substitutes, 7
Patterns. *See also* Coding of pattern pieces
  complete vs. half pieces, 27, 28
  envelopes for, 7–8
  file for, 7–8

ironing, 8
layout of, 26
notebook for, 8
tracing cloth for, 7
Pegged skirts, 62
Pellon, 7
Plackets, 58
Plaids, matching, 28
Pleats
  kick, 62
  pocket, 113–114
  skirt, 17, 62, 96–98
  trouser, 122–123
  unpressed, 145
Pockets, 29, 30, 37
  inseam, 32–34, 37, 111
  on skirts, 66, 78, 81
  patch, 37, 112–114
  placement, 28
  pleated, 113–114
  pouch, 41
  sewing, 38
Preshrinking of fabric, 134
Proportions, 99. *See also* Figure types
Pullover jackets, 56, 58

R
Remnants, 101
Reversible garments, 56, 79
Robes, 37
Ruffles, 42

S
Sashed waistbands, 124, 125
Sashes, obi, 59, 60
Seam allowances, 26, 56
Seams, 26, 38
Seam tape, 123
Self-image, 9, 10
Serge stitching, 26, 111, 135
Sewing room, organizing, 7
Shirts, set-in sleeved, 44–54
  back, 46–47
  collar, 55–56
  front, 48
  sleeves, 49–54
  survey questions, 45
  variations, 56–60
Shirtwaist dresses, 16, 145
Shorts, 136–138
Shoulders, jumpsuit openings at, 150
Shrinkage, fabric, 134
Side seams, sewing, 38
Silk, 42
  skirts, 65
Sizes, conversion of, 69

Skirts, 63–102
  A-line, 87
  altering, 98–100
  back, 71–73
  darts, 72–73
  denim, 64
  dirndl, 88–89
  front, 74–76
  golf, 101, 102
  gored, 95
  in business wardrobes, 64
  pleated, 96–97
  reversible, 79, 84
  sewing, 77
  silk, 65
  simplicity of sewing, 64–65
  straight, 62, 66
  styles of, 62, 63
  survey questions, 66–70
  tennis, 101, 102
  tulip, 90–94
  variations, 101–102
  wedding, 65
  wool tweed, 63
  wrap, 77–86
Sleeve(s)
  bell, 143
  capped, 24–43
  creating pattern for, 49–54
  cuffs, 45
  edge, 38
  kimono, 37
  roll-up, 59, 60
  set-in, 45–61
  straight, 62, 66
  tiered, 62
  top, 49, 53
  turning inside out of, 46
Slits, in ankle-length garments, 38
Snaps, 150, 151
Stitch-in-the-ditch, 32
Survey questions
  garment with capped sleeves, 25
  garment with set-in sleeves, 45
  skirts, 67
  pants, 104, 115
Sweat pants, 134

T
Tennis skirts, 101, 102
Tent dresses, 143, 144
Terry cloth, 38
Textures, fabric, 9
Tiered skirts, 62
Topstitching, 40, 59, 112
Trousers, 121–123
Tulip skirts, 90–94
Tulip sleeves, 143
Tunics, 25–34

U
Universal mill coding, 15

V
Velcro fastening tape, 124, 150
Vertical lines, 12, 13

W
Waistbands
  elastic, 101, 109
  pants, 120
  scarf-like, 124, 125
  skirt, 82–83, 99
  wrap, 124–129
Waist-hip proportions, 99
Waistlines
  indication on pattern of, 27
  pants, 111
  seams, 148–149
  skirt, 74–75
  tunic, 25
  variations, 36
Washing, of fabrics, 15
Wedding skirts, 65
Width adjusting, 66–70, 99–100
Windbreakers, 56, 57
Woven fabrics, 45, 103
  jumpsuits, 150–154
  pants, 115–120
Wrap pants, 124–129
Wrap skirts, 62, 77–86

Z
Zigzag stitching, 111, 120
Zippers
  jumpsuit, 150, 151
  pants, 117, 118, 119, 123